A SPIRITUAL GUIDE TO PRAYER AND BELIEF

How Faith and Prayer Lead to Wholeness

Nafeez Imtiaz

CONTENTS

Title Page

Copyright

Preface

Journeying Inward: Self-Discovery through Faith

The Healing Power of Gratitude: Transforming Your Mindset

The Interplay of Body, Mind, and Spirit: Holistic Healing Through Faith

Facing Adversity with Grace: How Faith Guides Us through Hardship

Spiritual Healing in Relationships: Mending Bonds through Prayer

The Language of the Heart: Crafting Personal Prayers

Epilogue

Afterword

PREFACE

In the hushed corners of ancient temples, the serene gardens of monasteries, and the quiet chambers of spiritual retreats across the globe, I embarked on a journey that would forever change my understanding of faith and prayer. As I sat with spiritual leaders, saints, and monks from diverse traditions, I found myself immersed in a world where the boundaries between the physical and the spiritual blurred, where words became bridges to the divine, and where silence spoke volumes.

This book, "A Spiritual Guide to Prayer and Belief," is not just a collection of teachings or a manual of prayer techniques. It is a living, breathing testament to the transformative power of faith and the profound impact of prayer on the human spirit. Through countless conversations, shared meals, and moments of quiet contemplation with spiritual guides from various corners of the world, I have woven together a tapestry of wisdom that transcends cultural and religious boundaries.

From the snow-capped mountains of Tibet to the sun-baked deserts of the Middle East, from the lush forests of South America to the bustling cities of Europe, I encountered individuals whose lives were dedicated to the pursuit of spiritual truth. Each of them, in their own unique way, demonstrated how faith and prayer could lead to a sense of wholeness – a state of being where the fragmented pieces of our existence come together in harmony.

As I listened to their stories and participated in their rituals, I found myself not just as an observer, but as a student, a seeker, and ultimately, a storyteller. The words you'll read in these pages are my humble attempt to capture the essence of these profound experiences and teachings. I've endeavored to convey not just the information shared, but the emotions felt, the energies experienced, and the transformations witnessed.

You'll meet a Buddhist monk whose daily practice of loving-kindness meditation has rippled out to touch thousands of lives. You'll hear from a Sufi mystic whose whirling dance is a prayer in motion, connecting earth and sky. You'll learn from an indigenous shaman whose prayers are whispered to the winds and carried to the ancestors. Each account is a window into a different facet of spiritual practice, yet all point to the same fundamental truth: that through faith and prayer, we can achieve a state of wholeness that transcends our individual limitations.

But this book is more than just a collection of other people's experiences. It's an invitation – an invitation to explore your own spiritual path, to deepen your own practice of prayer, and to discover your own journey towards wholeness. The wisdom shared here is not meant to be passively absorbed, but actively engaged with. It's my hope that as you read, you'll find yourself pausing, reflecting, and perhaps even praying in new ways.

In crafting this narrative, I've tried to strike a balance between honoring the original teachings and making them accessible to a modern audience. While the core messages remain true to their sources, I've taken the liberty of using language and analogies that I hope will resonate with readers from all walks of life. My aim is not to water down these profound teachings, but to present them in a way that invites deeper understanding and personal application.

As you embark on this journey through the pages of this book, I invite you to approach it with an open heart and an open mind. Whether you're a seasoned practitioner of a particular faith tradition, a curious seeker, or someone who's skeptical about spiritual matters, there's something here for you. The path to wholeness is not a one-size-fits-all journey, but a deeply personal exploration. Let the stories and teachings in this book be signposts on your own unique path.

In a world that often feels fragmented and chaotic, the promise of wholeness through faith and prayer is more relevant than ever. It's my sincere hope that this book will serve as a guide, a companion, and perhaps even a catalyst on your spiritual journey. May it inspire you to dive deeper into your own practice, to explore new ways of connecting with the divine, and to discover the transformative power of prayer in your own life.

Thank you for joining me on this extraordinary journey. May your own path to wholeness be filled with wonder, growth, and profound connection.

Nafeez Imtiaz

JOURNEYING INWARD: SELF-DISCOVERY THROUGH FAITH

Exploring Your Inner Self through Prayer

There's a deep stillness that comes when I close my eyes, bow my head, and feel the presence of something greater than myself. That stillness isn't silence—it's full of quiet anticipation, like the moments just before dawn when the world seems to be holding its breath. For me, prayer is that dawn. It's the spark that brings me back to my truest self, letting me slip past all the noise, all the self-doubt, and dive inward to meet myself in a space that feels both ancient and new.

When I first began truly exploring prayer, it was less about seeking answers and more about finding a place of refuge. Life was chaotic, and there was a constant buzz around me—emails to answer, goals to achieve, people to impress. But something always felt missing. I'd go about my days filled with ambition but empty of purpose, checking off lists but lacking that deep connection to myself. One evening, in the middle of this endless cycle, I found myself asking, "Who am I when all this fades away?" I realized then that I didn't fully know the answer.

It was with this question that I turned to prayer, not as a ritual but as a journey inward. My faith had always been a part of me, something I cherished but never fully delved into. Growing up, I was taught the words, the rituals, and the stories, but the meaning behind them seemed to escape me, like sunlight slipping through fingers. I wondered if prayer could be more than words spoken out loud, more than whispered hopes or requests for strength. Could it be, instead, a way to meet myself at a level beyond all the external labels I'd come to rely on?

Starting this journey, I decided to let go of any expectations. I wanted to enter each moment of prayer with openness and honesty. The first time I sat down, I didn't even know what I was going to say; I just let myself be silent, breathing in and out, letting thoughts come and go without holding onto them. It was strange at first, almost like meeting a stranger in the mirror. Yet, there was also a relief in not trying to be anything or anyone in those moments—no goals to chase, no roles to play.

Slowly, the initial awkwardness faded, and in its place, I felt a kind of familiarity, as though I were returning to a part of myself I had long forgotten. I remember one particular evening that changed the way I viewed prayer forever. I had been wrestling with doubts and fears about the future, weighed down by the unpredictability of life. So I sat down, closed my eyes, and instead of asking for guidance or solutions, I simply let myself feel everything. I acknowledged my fears, my sadness, and even my disappointments. For the first time, prayer became a space to release and accept, not to request or resist.

That moment taught me that prayer didn't have to be about asking for change but could also be about embracing what already is. I began to see prayer as a way to hold space for all parts of myself—the parts that were messy, uncertain, even frightened. It was liberating to bring my whole self into that space, knowing that I didn't need to hide anything from myself or from the divine. The comfort that flowed from those moments helped me understand that prayer was not just about reaching upward but also about grounding myself, connecting deeply to who I was, flaws and all.

In the days that followed, my prayers evolved. They weren't just conversations but explorations. Some days, I'd find myself expressing gratitude for the simple moments of life—a sunrise that painted the sky in soft pinks, a breeze that carried the scent of blooming flowers, the laughter of a loved one. Other times, I'd sit with emotions I couldn't quite name, just allowing myself to feel, to be, without judgment. Each time, I felt a little more connected to myself, as if layers were being gently peeled away, revealing something purer, closer to my essence.

This journey wasn't without its challenges, though. There were times when I questioned everything—when my faith felt fragile, like it could crumble at the slightest touch. I remember one particularly difficult period when I was going through personal struggles, and prayer felt empty, almost meaningless. Sitting there, I questioned everything I had come to believe. Why wasn't I feeling that comfort, that sense of connection? I doubted whether this inward journey was even real or just a hopeful illusion I had constructed.

But even in that darkness, something urged me to keep going, to sit in silence, to keep searching. It was during one of those difficult days, when I felt lost and alone, that a quiet thought surfaced: "You don't have to have all the answers to keep searching." I let those words sink in, and with them came a profound realization. I didn't need to know everything; I just needed to keep showing up, trusting that even in the silence, even in the uncertainty, I was moving closer to understanding myself.

With time, I began to notice changes—not only in the way I prayed but in the way I lived. I approached life with a greater sense of calm, finding that I was more patient, less prone to frustration. I had always been quick to react, often letting emotions control me. But now, after practicing this journey of self-discovery through prayer, I felt more rooted, more capable of observing my emotions without being consumed by them. I became more forgiving, not only of others but of myself. There was a new sense of compassion in the way I treated my own mistakes, understanding that I, too, was a work in progress, constantly learning, constantly growing.

One particularly meaningful experience stands out. A few months into this journey, I was visiting an old friend. We walked through a park together, talking about everything and nothing, and I realized how present I felt in that moment. Usually, my mind would wander, busy with thoughts of work or what needed to be done next. But that day, I felt entirely there, savoring the sounds of birds, the warmth of the sun, and the comfort of a familiar presence. It was as if prayer had taught me to find holiness in the ordinary, to recognize that these small, simple moments held as much spiritual weight as any grand revelation.

Prayer has become more than a practice; it's now a lens through which I view the world. In times of joy, I find myself offering a silent prayer of gratitude, acknowledging the abundance around me. And in moments of sorrow or doubt, I turn inward, finding solace in knowing that I am held by something greater than my worries. This inner journey has taught me that faith isn't about certainty or perfection. It's about being open, about embracing all of life—the beauty and the pain—with a heart willing to listen and learn.

Now, whenever I feel lost, I return to that inner sanctuary, that quiet space of prayer where I can lay down my worries and just be. It's in those moments that I remember who I truly am, not defined by my successes or failures, but as a soul on a journey, constantly rediscovering itself. And through each prayer, each quiet moment, I find a little more of myself, uncovering layers, seeing my spirit more clearly, and finding peace in the knowledge that this journey is endless, yet always leading me closer to home.

In this continuous journey of self-discovery, I've come to realize that prayer is more than a connection with the divine; it's a profound connection with myself. Through it, I have learned to be gentle with my heart, to honor my path, and to trust that the journey inward is the one that ultimately leads me to the truest version of myself. And while I may not have all the answers, I've found something even more valuable—a trust in the process, a comfort in the unknown, and a faith in the journey itself.

Understanding Your Spiritual Identity

The first time I truly felt the weight of my own existence, I was standing on the edge of a cliff, overlooking a vast, churning ocean. The wind whipped around me, carrying the scent of salt and possibility, and in that moment, I felt both infinitesimally small and cosmically significant. It was then that I realized my journey to understand my spiritual identity had begun in earnest.

My name isn't important, but my story might be. I'm just an ordinary person who embarked on an extraordinary journey of self-discovery through faith. This path has led me through valleys of doubt, mountains of revelation, and forests of confusion, but each step has brought me closer to understanding the essence of who I am on a spiritual level.

I grew up in a household where religion was more of a cultural tradition than a living, breathing practice. We attended services on major holidays, said grace before meals when grandma visited, and generally considered ourselves "good people." But there was always something missing, a hollow space within me that longed for deeper meaning and connection.

As a teenager, I rebelled against the rigid structures of organized religion, declaring myself an atheist and throwing myself into the pursuit of scientific knowledge. I thought I'd found the answer in cold, hard facts and empirical evidence. Yet, even as I excelled in my studies and built a successful career, that nagging emptiness persisted.

It wasn't until my late twenties, during a particularly challenging period in my life, that I began to reconsider my stance on spirituality. I had just gone through a painful breakup, lost my job due to company downsizing, and was feeling utterly lost and alone. One sleepless night, out of sheer desperation, I found myself whispering into the darkness, "If there's anyone or anything out there, I could really use some help."

To my surprise, I felt a sudden warmth wash over me, a sense of peace that I couldn't explain rationally. It wasn't a booming voice from the heavens or a miraculous vision, but a quiet, gentle assurance that I wasn't alone. This experience cracked open a door within me, one that I had kept firmly shut for years.

Intrigued and a bit unsettled by this encounter, I began to explore different spiritual practices and philosophies. I meditated with Buddhists, attended

Sufi whirling ceremonies, participated in Native American sweat lodges, and even spent a weekend at a silent Christian retreat. Each experience offered glimpses of something greater than myself, but none felt quite like home.

It was during a solo hiking trip in the mountains that I had my next significant spiritual breakthrough. I had been walking for hours, my mind racing with questions about my purpose and place in the universe. As I reached the summit of a particularly challenging peak, I was struck by the breathtaking beauty surrounding me. The vast expanse of sky, the rugged contours of the earth, the delicate wildflowers pushing through rocky soil – it all seemed to pulse with an energy I could feel but not see.

In that moment, I felt a profound connection to everything around me. It was as if the boundaries of my self-dissolved, and I could sense the interconnectedness of all life. This wasn't just an intellectual understanding, but a visceral, embodied experience that shook me to my core.

As I sat there, tears streaming down my face, I realized that my spiritual identity wasn't something I needed to find or create – it was something I needed to uncover. It had been there all along, buried beneath layers of societal conditioning, personal fears, and limiting beliefs.

From that day forward, my approach to spirituality changed dramatically. Instead of searching for answers outside myself, I began to look inward. I started a daily meditation practice, not to achieve any particular state of enlightenment, but simply to cultivate awareness and presence.

At first, sitting in silence was excruciating. My mind would race, my body would fidget, and I'd find myself peeking at the clock every few minutes. But slowly, with patience and persistence, I began to find moments of stillness. In these quiet spaces, I started to notice the subtle whispers of my inner voice, the one that had been drowned out by the noise of everyday life for so long.

This inner voice led me to explore my beliefs, values, and assumptions about life and my place in it. I began journaling regularly, pouring out my thoughts and feelings onto paper without judgment or censorship. Through this process, I uncovered deep-seated fears and limiting beliefs that had been shaping my perception of reality without my conscious awareness.

One particularly powerful realization came when I was reflecting on my childhood. I remembered a time when, as a young child, I had expressed a desire to become an artist. My well-meaning parents had gently steered me towards more "practical" pursuits, telling me that art was a nice hobby but not a viable career. As I wrote about this memory, I suddenly understood how this early experience had shaped my belief that creativity and spirituality were luxuries, not essential parts of a meaningful life.

Armed with this insight, I began to give myself permission to explore my creative side as part of my spiritual practice. I took up painting, not with the goal of becoming a professional artist, but as a form of meditation and self-expression. As I mixed colors and applied them to canvas, I found myself entering a state of flow that felt deeply spiritual. The act of creation became a way of connecting with something greater than myself, of channeling energy and inspiration from a source I couldn't fully explain but could definitely feel.

As my spiritual journey deepened, I also began to notice changes in my relationships with others. I found myself becoming more patient, more compassionate, and more present in my interactions. Instead of getting caught up in petty disagreements or taking things personally, I was able to step back and see the bigger picture. I realized that everyone is on their own journey, facing their own challenges and carrying their own burdens.

This shift in perspective led me to volunteer at a local homeless shelter. I went in thinking I would be the one giving help, but I quickly discovered that I had just as much to learn from the people I was serving. One evening, I had a conversation with an elderly man named Tom who had been living on the streets for years. As he shared his story with me, I was struck by the wisdom and resilience he had gained through his struggles. Tom taught me that spiritual growth often comes through adversity, and that true strength lies in maintaining one's humanity in the face of hardship.

My understanding of my spiritual identity continued to evolve as I explored different practices and teachings. I discovered the power of gratitude, making it a point to acknowledge the blessings in my life each day, no matter how small. This simple practice shifted my focus from what was lacking to what was abundant, and I found my overall sense of wellbeing improving dramatically.

I also delved into the study of sacred texts from various traditions, not to adopt any one belief system wholesale, but to glean universal truths that resonated with my own experiences. I was fascinated to find common threads running through seemingly disparate teachings – the importance of love and compassion, the interconnectedness of all things, and the power of surrendering to a higher purpose.

One practice that had a profound impact on my spiritual growth was spending time in nature. I made it a point to regularly disconnect from technology and immerse myself in the natural world. Whether it was a walk in the local park, a weekend camping trip, or simply sitting in my backyard observing the birds and insects, these experiences helped me feel more grounded and connected to the rhythms of life.

During one such nature retreat, I had an experience that further deepened my understanding of my spiritual identity. I was sitting by a stream, watching the water flow over rocks and around obstacles, when I had a sudden insight. Just as the water adapted to the contours of the landscape while maintaining its essential nature, I too could flow through life's challenges without losing my core self. This realization helped me navigate difficult situations with more grace and flexibility, trusting in my innate ability to adapt while staying true to my spiritual essence.

As my journey progressed, I began to understand that my spiritual identity wasn't something fixed or static, but a dynamic, evolving aspect of myself. It wasn't about adhering to a specific set of beliefs or practices, but about cultivating a deep, authentic connection with myself, others, and the world around me.

This understanding was put to the test when I faced a major health scare. Doctors had found a suspicious mass, and for weeks, I lived with the uncertainty of not knowing whether I was seriously ill. In the past, such a situation would have sent me into a spiral of fear and anxiety. But drawing on the spiritual resources I had cultivated, I was able to face this challenge with a sense of peace and trust.

During sleepless nights, I turned to meditation and prayer, not asking for any specific outcome, but simply opening myself to whatever lessons this experience had to offer. I found comfort in the knowledge that my worth as a person wasn't tied to my physical health or any external circumstances. My spiritual identity, I realized, transcended the temporary conditions of my body and mind.

Thankfully, the mass turned out to be benign, but the experience left an indelible mark on my spiritual journey. It deepened my appreciation for the preciousness of life and reinforced my commitment to living each day with intention and gratitude.

As I continued to explore and deepen my understanding of my spiritual identity, I found myself naturally drawn to share my experiences with others. I didn't set out to become a teacher or guru – far from it. But as I opened up about my journey, I found that many people were grappling with similar questions and challenges.

I started hosting small gatherings in my home, where we would meditate together, discuss spiritual topics, and support each other in our individual journeys. These meetings became a rich source of community and mutual growth. I learned as much from listening to others' experiences as I did from sharing my own.

One particularly memorable evening, a young woman in our group shared her struggle with forgiveness. She had been deeply hurt by a family member and found herself unable to move past the pain and anger. As we sat in circle, each person offered their perspective and support. I shared my own experience with forgiveness, how I had come to see it not as a one-time act, but as an ongoing process of releasing and renewing.

As we talked, I could see a shift happening in the young woman's eyes. She didn't have a miraculous breakthrough that night, but she left with a new perspective and a sense of hope. Witnessing her process reminded me of the power of community in spiritual growth and reinforced my belief that we are all teachers and students for each other.

Through these shared experiences, I came to understand that my spiritual identity wasn't just about my individual relationship with the divine or the universe. It was also about my connection to and responsibility towards others. I realized that true spiritual growth isn't just about personal enlightenment, but about how we show up in the world and contribute to the wellbeing of all.

This realization led me to become more involved in social justice issues, seeing them as an extension of my spiritual practice. I participated in peaceful protests, volunteered for organizations working to address systemic inequalities, and sought to educate myself about the experiences of marginalized communities. These activities weren't separate from my spiritual journey – they were an integral part of it, challenging me to put my beliefs into action and to see the divine in every person, especially those society often overlooks or devalues.

As I reflect on my journey of understanding my spiritual identity, I'm struck by how far I've come from that confused, empty person I once was. Yet at the same time, I recognize that this journey is far from over. In fact, I've come to see that it's not about reaching a final destination of complete understanding or enlightenment. Rather, it's about embracing the journey itself, with all its twists and turns, challenges and revelations.

My spiritual identity, I've learned, is not something that can be definitively pinned down or fully articulated. It's a living, breathing aspect of who I am, constantly evolving as I grow and change. It's the quiet voice that guides me towards compassion when I'm tempted to judge. It's the sense of awe I feel when I witness a beautiful sunset or the miracle of a new life being born. It's the courage that wells up within me when I'm called to stand up for what's right, even when it's difficult.

Understanding my spiritual identity has been like peeling an onion – each layer revealed has led to deeper insights and new questions. It's a process that has brought tears of both joy and pain, moments of profound clarity and periods of confusing darkness. But through it all, I've come to trust in the journey itself, to have faith in the unfolding of my own unique spiritual path.

As I write these words, I'm aware that my understanding will likely shift and deepen in the days, months, and years to come. And that's okay. In fact, it's more than okay – it's exciting. Because I've learned that the quest to understand one's spiritual identity is not about arriving at a fixed destination, but about embracing the beautiful, messy, awe-inspiring journey of becoming more fully ourselves.

To anyone embarking on their own journey of spiritual self-discovery, I offer this advice: Be patient with yourself. Trust the process. Stay open to unexpected lessons and teachers. And remember, your spiritual identity is not something you need to create or force – it's already there within you, waiting to be uncovered and expressed in your own unique way.

The journey inward is not always easy, but it is infinitely rewarding. It's a journey that can transform not only your own life but ripple out to touch the lives of those around you. So take that first step, or the next step, or a thousand more steps on your path of self-discovery through faith. The journey of understanding your spiritual identity is the journey of a lifetime – and it starts anew with each moment, each breath, and each choice to turn inward and listen to the whispers of your soul.

Faith as a Mirror for Self-Reflection

Faith has often felt like a mirror reflecting the depths of my soul, showing me not just who I am, but who I aspire to be. I remember the first time I truly recognized this connection between faith and self-reflection. I sat in a quiet corner of my home, a cozy nook filled with soft pillows and the scent of sandalwood wafting through the air. It was a rainy afternoon, and the world outside felt distant. I closed my eyes and allowed myself to sink into the stillness, craving a moment of solitude where I could explore my thoughts.

In that silence, I began to contemplate the beliefs that shaped my life. I had always held faith close to my heart, but I realized that I had often viewed it as something external—a set of doctrines or principles to which I adhered. That day, however, I started to see it as a living, breathing entity that invited me to look inward. I asked myself, "What does my faith reveal about me?" As I pondered this question, I felt a gentle stirring within, urging me to dive deeper.

The journey inward is rarely straightforward. At first, I encountered uncomfortable truths about myself. I had always prided myself on my kindness and generosity, yet I found moments when I had acted out of frustration or selfishness. I recalled a recent interaction where I had snapped at a friend during a vulnerable moment. As I reflected on that incident, I felt a wave of shame wash over me. I had let my emotions cloud my judgment, and in that moment, I realized that my faith called me to something greater —to embody compassion and understanding even when it felt challenging.

Recognizing this dissonance between my actions and my beliefs stirred a desire for growth within me. I began to see faith not just as a set of beliefs but as a call to action. I embraced the idea that my faith could guide me toward becoming a better version of myself. I decided to meditate on the qualities I wanted to cultivate—patience, empathy, and humility. Each evening, I would sit quietly, repeating affirmations that resonated with my intentions. "I am patient. I am compassionate. I am open to growth." These words became a mantra, echoing in my heart as I navigated daily life.

As I continued this inward journey, I noticed how faith provided me with a framework for understanding my experiences. I started to view challenges as opportunities for reflection and growth. One day, I faced a difficult situation at work. A project I had poured my heart into fell apart due to unforeseen complications. Frustration bubbled within me, and I felt the urge to blame others. But I paused, remembering my commitment to self-reflection. Instead of reacting impulsively, I took a step back and asked myself what this experience was teaching me.

In that moment, I realized that my faith encouraged me to embrace vulnerability. I acknowledged my disappointment and allowed myself to feel it fully. But I also recognized that this setback didn't define me. I prayed for clarity, asking for wisdom in navigating the situation. After some contemplation, I decided to reach out to my colleagues and engage in a constructive dialogue. This act of humility not only helped mend relationships but also strengthened my resolve to move forward with grace.

Many evenings afterward, I continued to sit in reflection, allowing my faith to guide me through difficult emotions. I often thought about the concept of forgiveness, both for myself and others. I recalled the times I had held onto grudges, feeling justified in my anger. But faith, in its gentle way, nudged me to reconsider. I began to understand that forgiveness was not about condoning hurtful actions; it was about freeing myself from the weight of resentment.

One night, while sitting in my cozy nook, I reflected on a past relationship that had ended badly. I had carried the bitterness of that breakup for far too long, allowing it to taint my perception of love and connection. I closed my eyes and envisioned the person I had once cared for, recalling the good moments we shared alongside the pain. As I prayed, I felt a shift within me. I recognized that holding onto anger only kept me tethered to the past. I decided to release that burden, not for them, but for myself. In that moment of surrender, I felt lighter, as if a heavy weight had been lifted from my shoulders.

Through these reflections, I also discovered the beauty of gratitude. I realized that faith often flourished in moments of appreciation. I began a nightly practice of writing down three things I was grateful for each evening. At first, I struggled to find significant moments to highlight, but soon I learned to appreciate the small joys—like the warmth of my morning coffee, the laughter of friends, or the beauty of a sunset. This practice nurtured a sense of abundance in my life, reminding me that even in tough times, there was always something to be thankful for.

One evening, as I sat reflecting on my day, I noticed how my faith had shifted my perspective on challenges. I had faced a particularly difficult conversation with a family member, one that had left me feeling drained. Yet, rather than focusing on the discomfort, I reflected on the courage it took to have that conversation. I felt proud of myself for addressing the issue openly and honestly. Faith had helped me recognize that vulnerability could lead to deeper connections, even when it felt daunting.

As I journeyed deeper into self-reflection, I also began to explore the concept of purpose. Faith encouraged me to ask questions about my life's direction. I often found myself pondering the impact I wanted to have on the world. One afternoon, while journaling, I wrote, "What legacy do I wish to leave behind?" This question ignited a spark within me. I envisioned a life dedicated to service, to uplifting others and making a difference in my community.

Inspired by this newfound clarity, I began volunteering at a local organization that supported underprivileged families. The experience was transformative. As I immersed myself in service, I discovered joy in giving. I felt a deep sense of connection to the people I served, and I realized that my faith was manifesting through my actions. Each time I offered support or a listening ear, I felt my heart expand. I understood that faith was not just about belief; it was about embodying those beliefs in the world.

Throughout this journey, I also encountered moments of doubt. There were times when I questioned my faith, searching for answers to life's complexities. During one particularly challenging period, I faced a series of setbacks that left me feeling disheartened. My usual sense of clarity wavered, and I found myself grappling with feelings of confusion. I turned to my evening reflections, seeking solace in the familiar practice. I prayed for guidance, for the strength to navigate uncertainty.

In those moments of vulnerability, I learned that doubt was a natural part of the journey. I began to embrace it as an opportunity for growth rather than a weakness. I realized that questioning my beliefs didn't diminish my faith; it deepened my understanding. I sought out literature and conversations that challenged my perspective, allowing me to expand my horizons. I learned that the journey inward is not always smooth, but it is essential for self-discovery.

As I continued to reflect on my experiences, I became more aware of the interconnectedness of all things. I began to see how my thoughts, actions, and beliefs were woven into the fabric of the universe. One evening, while contemplating the beauty of nature, I felt a profound sense of unity with the world around me. I closed my eyes and listened to the sounds of the evening—the rustling of leaves, the chirping of crickets, the distant hum of life. In that moment, I felt a deep connection to everything, as if my faith was a thread binding us all together.

This realization sparked a desire to express my gratitude for the interconnectedness of life. I started to integrate mindfulness into my daily routine, taking moments to pause and appreciate the beauty around me. Whether it was during a walk in the park or while sipping my morning tea, I would take a moment to breathe and connect with the present. These small acts of mindfulness enriched my experience, reminding me that faith is a living, breathing energy that flows through everything.

As I journeyed further into self-discovery through faith, I began to share my insights with others. I realized that my experiences could serve as a source of inspiration for those around me. I started facilitating small group discussions, inviting friends to share their own journeys of faith and self-reflection. Together, we created a space where vulnerability was welcomed, and deep conversations flourished. I found joy in witnessing others connect with their own truths, recognizing that faith serves as a mirror for us all.

Through these discussions, I discovered the power of storytelling. Each person brought their unique experiences, and as we shared, I felt the threads of connection weaving us closer together. I began to understand that faith is not a solitary journey; it is enriched by community and shared experiences. I learned that in sharing our struggles and triumphs, we create a tapestry of understanding and support.

One evening, a friend shared her story of grappling with loss. She spoke of the deep pain she had felt and how her faith had been tested. As she shared, I felt tears welling in my eyes. Her vulnerability resonated deeply within me, and I realized that we all face moments of darkness. I offered my support, and in that exchange, I felt a sense of unity. It reinforced my belief that faith serves as a mirror, reflecting our shared humanity.

As the seasons changed, so did my journey of self-discovery through faith. I embraced the cyclical nature of life, recognizing that each phase brought new opportunities for reflection and growth. I found beauty in the ebb and flow, allowing myself to be present in each moment. I learned to celebrate the small victories, to honor the lessons learned, and to be gentle with myself during challenging times.

Eventually, I began to notice a profound shift in my perspective. Faith had become a guiding light, illuminating my path and encouraging me to embrace my true self. I felt empowered to live authentically, to pursue my passions, and to nurture my relationships. Each evening, as I sat in reflection, I expressed gratitude for the journey—the moments of doubt, the triumphs, and the lessons learned along the way.

In closing, I invite you to explore the transformative power of faith as a mirror for self-reflection. Embrace the journey inward, allowing your beliefs to guide you toward self-discovery and growth. Create space for vulnerability, for questioning, and for connection with others. Recognize that faith is not just an external concept; it is a living energy that flows through you and the world around you. Together, let us celebrate the journey of self-discovery through faith, honoring the beauty of our shared humanity and the profound insights that emerge along the way.

Navigating the Depths of the Soul

There's something magical about the moment you decide to look inward, to turn away from the distractions around you and journey into the depths of your own soul. It's not an easy choice, and it's certainly not comfortable, but I found that it's one of the most profound gifts I could ever give myself. As I ventured inward, I discovered not just layers of old experiences and emotions but also glimmers of a truth that felt deeply familiar, as if it had been waiting for me all along.

I can still remember when this journey first began. It wasn't planned or part of any grand vision I had for myself. Rather, it started on a night that felt endless, during a time in my life when I was surrounded by noise yet felt isolated. I had always kept busy, filling my time with goals, obligations, and even a little bit of escapism. I thought that if I kept moving, if I stayed productive, I'd never have to confront the restless unease within me. But on that particular night, there was nowhere to go, and the silence was almost deafening.

It felt like the universe was nudging me, whispering, "It's time." And for reasons I couldn't fully understand, I found myself wanting to listen. I sat down, closed my eyes, and decided to look into myself instead of looking away. I expected it to be uncomfortable, even painful, but the feeling was different. It was almost like finally meeting someone I'd been avoiding for years—a stranger who somehow knew me better than I knew myself.

As I sat there, I noticed my mind filling with questions that I had never dared to ask. Who am I beneath all these roles I play? Who am I when I strip away my career, my relationships, my achievements, and even my failures? The deeper I dug, the more questions seemed to arise, and they were questions that didn't come with easy answers. But something in me felt determined to understand, to keep going no matter what I found.

One of the earliest realizations I had was that I'd been carrying a lot more than I knew. There were old pains, regrets, and fears that I had buried so deep that I had almost forgotten they were there. But as I allowed myself to sit with them, to look at them directly, I began to feel a strange relief. It was like taking off a heavy coat I hadn't realized I was wearing. I didn't need to run from these parts of myself; I simply needed to acknowledge them, to accept them as a part of my story.

I found myself recalling a specific memory from my early adulthood. It was a time when I felt intensely vulnerable and lost, overwhelmed by the expectations I'd placed on myself. In that memory, I was struggling to live up to what I thought I needed to be, wearing a mask to shield my insecurities. For so long, I had held onto that version of myself, believing that those feelings of inadequacy were still a part of who I was. But as I sat in silence, I realized that I wasn't that person anymore. I could let go of that memory and the grip it held on me.

Releasing that part of my past felt like a healing, as though I was mending a wound I hadn't even known was there. I learned that I didn't need to define myself by those difficult moments. Instead, I could view them as stepping stones, reminders of my resilience and growth. This was one of the first breakthroughs in my journey inward—the realization that my past did not define me; it only illuminated the path I had walked to reach where I was now.

As the weeks passed, I became more comfortable with the stillness. Instead of a ritual or routine, my time of introspection became a sacred space—a place where I could meet myself without pretense. And as I grew more comfortable with my own presence, I began to explore parts of myself I had never dared to examine. Some days, I would sit in quiet reflection, allowing whatever emotions arose to simply be there. Other days, I'd ask myself questions that seemed to come from some hidden place within me.

One of those questions, one that I can still remember vividly, was, "What am I afraid to see?" At first, I didn't know how to answer. But as I sat with it, images and feelings began to surface—fear of failure, fear of being seen as inadequate, even fear of being truly happy. It was startling to realize that some part of me was afraid of the very things I had always said I wanted. I wondered how many dreams I had kept at arm's length, simply because I was too afraid to let them in.

One particular experience stands out from those early days. I remember sitting alone by a lake one afternoon, a place I had always gone to clear my mind. I watched the ripples in the water, noticing how they expanded outward, touching every corner of the lake. It struck me that my soul was much like that lake, with emotions and thoughts creating ripples that reached far beyond my conscious awareness. As I watched those ripples, I felt a strange kinship with the water—a realization that just as the lake held both calm and turbulence, so did I. And that was okay. I didn't need to be perfect or to have all the answers; I just needed to be present with myself, to let the ripples move as they would.

With time, I began to see that these journeys inward, these quiet explorations of my soul, were not about fixing myself. They weren't about becoming someone different or escaping my flaws. Instead, they were about meeting myself with compassion, about seeing the beauty in the parts of myself that I had once deemed unworthy or broken. Each moment spent in reflection was like another piece of a puzzle coming together, revealing a picture that was far more intricate and beautiful than I had ever imagined.

In the course of this journey, I also found myself becoming more compassionate toward others. I had always believed that understanding myself was a solitary journey, one that wouldn't affect the people around me. But as I explored my own soul, I became more aware of the struggles others faced, the burdens they carried quietly. I started to listen more, to hold space for others the way I had learned to hold space for myself. This was an unexpected gift of my inward journey—the realization that by knowing myself, I could connect more deeply with those around me.

There was one evening not too long ago that brought all of these realizations into sharp focus. I had been feeling particularly reflective, contemplating all that I had learned about myself over the years. I decided to take a walk through a nearby forest, hoping to find clarity in the midst of nature's quiet beauty. As I walked, I found myself marveling at the trees, their branches reaching skyward, and their roots deep in the earth. I felt a profound sense of connection, a reminder that just like those trees, I too had roots, and I too reached toward something greater than myself.

In that moment, I felt as if I had come full circle. This journey inward had led me not to a destination but to an ongoing discovery, a process that would continue as long as I was willing to embrace it. I realized that my soul, like the forest, was full of hidden paths, places waiting to be explored. And I felt at peace, knowing that each step I took was not an ending but a new beginning, a chance to know myself a little better, to understand my place in the world with a little more clarity.

This journey has taught me many things, but perhaps the most important lesson is that the soul is not something to be conquered or understood in a single moment. It is a living, breathing part of who we are, constantly evolving, and constantly revealing itself in new ways. The depths of the soul are vast and endless, a mystery that cannot be solved but only embraced.

I still sit with myself in silence, still ask questions, and still let myself feel whatever arises. Each time, I discover something new, something I hadn't seen before. And I am grateful, not just for the answers but for the questions, for the journey itself. This path inward, this exploration of my soul, has shown me that I am more than I ever knew, that within me exists a depth and beauty that no words could fully capture.

And so, I keep journeying inward, knowing that with each step, I am moving closer to the essence of who I am, finding peace not in certainty but in the wonder of discovery. It's a journey without end, and I am thankful for every moment of it. In the depths of my soul, I have found a place that is both familiar and forever new—a place that, no matter where life leads, I can always return to.

Discovering Your True Purpose

The day I realized I had been living someone else's life was the day my world turned upside down. I stood in front of the mirror, staring at a stranger wearing my face, and I knew something had to change. That moment marked the beginning of my journey to discover my true purpose —a journey that would lead me through the depths of despair, the heights of joy, and ultimately, to a profound understanding of myself and my place in the world.

My name isn't important, but my story might resonate with you. I'm just an ordinary person who dared to ask the big questions: Why am I here? What am I meant to do with my life? How can I make a meaningful contribution to the world? These questions set me on a path of self-discovery through faith that I never could have anticipated.

Growing up, I did everything I was supposed to do. I got good grades, went to a prestigious university, landed a high-paying job in finance, and bought a house in the suburbs. On paper, I had achieved the American dream. But inside, I felt hollow. Each day, I'd wake up with a gnawing sense of emptiness, go through the motions at work, and come home feeling drained and unfulfilled.

I tried to fill the void with material possessions, relationships, and achievements, but nothing seemed to work. It wasn't until I hit rock bottom —burned out, depressed, and contemplating quitting my job without a plan —that I realized something had to give.

One sleepless night, I found myself on my knees, tears streaming down my face, crying out to a God I wasn't sure I believed in. "Please," I whispered into the darkness, "show me why I'm here. Help me find my purpose." In that moment of complete surrender, I felt a shift. It wasn't dramatic or earth-shattering, but a subtle warmth that spread through my chest, like a gentle embrace.

That night marked the beginning of my spiritual awakening. I began to explore different faith traditions, not with the goal of finding the "right" one, but with an open heart and mind, eager to learn and grow. I meditated with Buddhists, prayed with Christians, chanted with Hindus, and sat in silence with Quakers. Each experience offered valuable insights, but none felt quite like home.

It was during a solo retreat in nature that I had my first significant breakthrough. I had spent three days alone in a small cabin in the woods, fasting and meditating. On the third day, as I sat by a stream watching the water flow over rocks, I had a profound realization: my purpose wasn't something I needed to find or create, but something I needed to uncover. Like the stream finding its natural path through the forest, my true purpose was already within me, waiting to be revealed.

This insight sparked a shift in my approach. Instead of looking outside myself for answers, I began to turn inward. I started a daily practice of meditation and journaling, creating space to listen to my inner voice—the one that had been drowned out by society's expectations and my own fears for so long.

At first, this inner work was challenging. I'd sit down to meditate, and my mind would race with thoughts about work, relationships, and all the things I "should" be doing. But gradually, with patience and persistence, I began to find moments of stillness. In these quiet spaces, I started to hear whispers of my true self, nudging me towards a life of greater authenticity and purpose.

One pivotal moment came during a particularly deep meditation session. As I sat in silence, I had a vivid vision of myself as a child, full of curiosity and wonder, exploring the world with wide-eyed enthusiasm. I saw how that childlike joy had been slowly eroded by years of conforming to others' expectations. In that moment, I made a commitment to reconnect with that part of myself—to rediscover what truly brought me joy and fulfillment.

Armed with this new awareness, I began to make small changes in my life. I started saying "no" to obligations that didn't align with my values and "yes" to experiences that sparked my curiosity. I took up painting again, a passion I had abandoned in college because it wasn't "practical." I volunteered at a local animal shelter, rediscovering my love for animals and the satisfaction of making a difference in their lives.

These small steps led to bigger ones. I reduced my hours at work to make time for volunteer projects and creative pursuits. I started having honest conversations with friends and family about my evolving beliefs and values. Some relationships grew stronger, while others naturally fell away as I became more aligned with my true self.

One of the most significant changes came when I decided to take a sabbatical from my job to travel and explore different cultures. This wasn't an easy decision—I was leaving behind a secure income and a clear career path. But something inside me knew it was necessary for my growth.

During my travels, I had experiences that profoundly shaped my understanding of my purpose. In a small village in Thailand, I spent time with a community that lived simply but joyfully, their lives centered on connection with each other and nature. This experience challenged my assumptions about success and happiness, showing me that true fulfillment comes not from external achievements, but from living in alignment with one's values and contributing to the wellbeing of others.

In India, I spent time in an ashram, diving deep into spiritual practices and philosophical discussions. It was here that I had a powerful realization about the nature of purpose itself. I came to understand that my purpose wasn't a single, fixed thing, but a dynamic expression of my highest self in each moment. This shift in perspective freed me from the pressure of trying to figure out one grand purpose for my life and allowed me to focus on living purposefully in the present.

Returning home after my travels, I felt like a different person. The old life I had left behind no longer fit, like a suit I had outgrown. I knew I couldn't go back to my corporate job, but I wasn't sure what was next. This period of uncertainty was both exciting and terrifying. I had to trust that if I continued to follow my inner guidance, the path would reveal itself.

And reveal itself it did, though not in the way I expected. One day, while volunteering at a youth center, I found myself naturally falling into the role of a mentor. As I listened to the young people share their dreams and fears, I felt a deep sense of resonance. I realized that my own journey of self-discovery had equipped me with insights and experiences that could be valuable to others on similar paths.

This realization led me to explore coaching and counseling as potential career paths. I enrolled in a coaching certification program, not knowing exactly where it would lead but trusting that it was the right next step. The training process was transformative, challenging me to confront my own limiting beliefs and deepen my self-awareness even further.

As I began working with clients, I was continually amazed by the power of holding space for others to explore their own purpose and potential. Each session felt like a sacred exchange, where I was both guide and student, learning as much from my clients as they were from me. I found myself naturally integrating spiritual principles into my coaching practice, helping clients connect with their own inner wisdom and higher purpose.

One particularly memorable client was a successful entrepreneur who came to me feeling empty and disconnected from his work. As we explored his values and passions, he reconnected with a childhood dream of becoming a teacher. Over several months, I supported him as he transitioned out of his business and into a new career in education. Witnessing his transformation—the light returning to his eyes as he found work that truly aligned with his purpose—was profoundly fulfilling.

As my coaching practice grew, I felt called to share my insights with a wider audience. I started writing about my experiences and the lessons I'd learned on my journey of self-discovery. What began as a personal blog evolved into a book project, allowing me to reach and inspire even more people?

Throughout this process, my understanding of my own purpose continued to evolve. I came to see that my role was not to have all the answers, but to ask powerful questions that could help others uncover their own truth. My purpose was to be a catalyst for transformation, creating spaces—whether in one-on-one coaching sessions, group workshops, or through my writing —where people could connect with their authentic selves and discover their unique gifts to share with the world.

This realization brought a deep sense of peace and alignment. I no longer felt the need to prove myself or achieve external markers of success. Instead, I found joy in the simple act of showing up each day, ready to serve and grow.

Of course, discovering my true purpose didn't mean that life became perfect or easy. I still faced challenges, doubts, and moments of uncertainty. But I had developed a strong inner compass that helped me navigate these difficulties with greater grace and resilience.

One particularly challenging period came when I faced a health crisis that forced me to slow down and reevaluate my priorities once again. Initially, I struggled against this limitation, feeling frustrated that I couldn't work at the pace I was accustomed to. But as I sat with this experience, I realized it was an invitation to deepen my practice of presence and self-compassion.

During my recovery, I discovered new ways to express my purpose that didn't require as much physical energy. I started a podcast where I could share inspiring stories and insights from my bed. I deepened my meditation practice, finding that I could be of service simply by holding space and sending positive intentions to the world.

This experience taught me that living my purpose wasn't about constant doing, but about being—being present, being authentic, and being open to the lessons each moment has to offer. I learned that sometimes, the most powerful way to fulfill our purpose is simply to embody the qualities we wish to see in the world: love, compassion, wisdom, and joy.

As I reflect on my journey of discovering my true purpose, I'm struck by how different my life looks now compared to where I started. Gone is the corporate job, the suburban house, the relentless pursuit of external success. In their place is a life rich with meaning, connection, and alignment with my deepest values.

But what's most remarkable is not the external changes, but the internal shift. I no longer feel like I'm living someone else's life or trying to fit into a mold that doesn't suit me. Instead, I wake up each day with a sense of excitement about how I can express my purpose in new and creative ways.

I've come to understand that discovering our true purpose is not a one-time event, but an ongoing journey of self-discovery and growth. It's about continually aligning our actions with our highest values and deepest truths. It's about being willing to let go of who we think we should be to become who we truly are.

To anyone embarking on their own journey of purpose discovery, I offer this advice: Be patient with yourself. Trust the process, even when it feels uncomfortable or uncertain. Stay open to unexpected possibilities and lessons. And remember, your purpose is not something you need to create or force—it's already within you, waiting to be uncovered and expressed in your own unique way.

The journey of discovering your true purpose is ultimately a journey of coming home to yourself. It's about peeling away the layers of conditioning and expectation to reveal the beautiful, authentic core of who you are. It's about recognizing that you are here for a reason, that your presence on this earth matters, and that you have unique gifts to share with the world.

As you embark on or continue your own journey of self-discovery through faith, know that you are not alone. Each step you take towards living your purpose not only transforms your own life but ripples out to touch the lives of others in ways you may never fully know. Trust in the unfolding of your path, listen to the whispers of your soul, and have faith that as you align with your true purpose, you are contributing to the healing and evolution of our world in profound and beautiful ways.

THE HEALING POWER OF GRATITUDE: TRANSFORMING YOUR MINDSET

Understanding the Role of Gratitude in Healing

Understanding the role of gratitude in healing has profoundly transformed my life in ways I never anticipated. I remember the day it all began. I sat on my bed, feeling the weight of the world pressing down on my shoulders. Life had thrown a series of curveballs my way—job stress, relationship struggles, and an undercurrent of anxiety that seemed to shadow my every move. I felt trapped in a cycle of negativity, and I yearned for a way out. That afternoon, I stumbled upon a simple idea that would change everything: gratitude.

Initially, I was skeptical. How could something as simple as listing things I was thankful for shift my mindset? But desperation often leads us to try unconventional methods. So, I decided to give it a shot. I grabbed a notebook and wrote down three things I was grateful for that day. As I sat there, pen in hand, I struggled to find anything meaningful. I wrote "my morning coffee" and "the sunshine." Even those felt trivial in the face of my overwhelming emotions. Yet, as I paused to reflect, I noticed a flicker of warmth in my heart. That little exercise opened a door I didn't know existed.

The next day, I repeated the exercise, and something magical happened. I found myself looking for moments to appreciate throughout the day. I noticed the way the sunlight filtered through the trees while I walked to work, casting playful shadows on the ground. I savored the laughter of a friend as we shared stories over lunch. Each time I wrote in my gratitude journal, I felt a small shift within me, as if my heart was lightening just a little more.

As the weeks went by, I began to observe the broader impact of gratitude on my healing process. I still faced challenges, but my perspective started to change. I began to see obstacles as opportunities for growth. One evening, while reflecting on a difficult conversation I had with a colleague, I realized how grateful I was for the chance to communicate openly. Instead of dwelling on the discomfort of that interaction, I focused on the courage it took to express my thoughts honestly. This newfound lens of gratitude helped me navigate my relationships with greater ease.

During this period, I experienced a significant emotional setback. I had been feeling particularly anxious, and the weight of unresolved issues loomed heavily over me. I found myself spiraling into negative thoughts, replaying past mistakes and worries about the future. It was then that I turned to my gratitude practice again. I recalled a suggestion I had read about focusing on gratitude in times of distress. One evening, I sat with my journal, determined to find light amid the darkness.

I wrote about small moments from the day, such as the comforting embrace of my favorite blanket and the warmth of my dog curled up beside me. I reflected on the unwavering support of my family, who had always been there for me during tough times. As I wrote, I felt tears streaming down my face, but they were not solely tears of sadness; they were tears of release. Gratitude became the balm for my wounds, helping me process my emotions more effectively.

This experience taught me that gratitude is not merely about acknowledging the good; it's about embracing the entirety of our experiences, including the painful ones. I began to see my struggles as valuable teachers. I often reflected on how healing isn't linear; it ebbs and flows, much like the tides.

Each wave of emotion, whether joy or sorrow, contributed to the mosaic of my life.

Another pivotal moment arose when I faced a health scare. I remember sitting in the waiting room, my heart racing and mind racing even faster. I felt a rush of anxiety wash over me as I anticipated the doctor's news. In that moment, I realized I needed to ground myself. I closed my eyes and took a deep breath. I recalled my gratitude practice, and instead of spiraling into fear, I focused on what I could appreciate in that moment. I was grateful for the medical professionals who dedicated their lives to helping others. I appreciated the love and support of my friends who had accompanied me that day. Even the simple act of being able to breathe deeply became a focal point of gratitude.

As the doctor entered the room, I held onto that sense of gratitude as a shield against fear. When I received the news, my heart sank, but I felt a spark of resilience ignite within me. I understood that while the news was challenging, I still had the power to choose how I responded. I realized that gratitude could coexist with fear and uncertainty, painting a more nuanced picture of my reality.

In the weeks that followed, I leaned heavily on my gratitude practice. I began to appreciate the small victories—every step I took toward healing, every moment of laughter shared with friends, and every sunrise that greeted me with new possibilities. I found comfort in knowing that healing is a journey, not a destination. Each day presented an opportunity to cultivate gratitude, allowing me to shift my focus from what I lacked to what I had.

One evening, I decided to host a gratitude gathering with close friends. I wanted to create a space where we could all share our experiences and express our thankfulness. As we sat in a circle, candles flickering and laughter filling the air, I felt a sense of community envelop us. Each person shared their stories, recounting moments of joy, struggle, and growth. I realized that gratitude was not just an individual practice; it flourished in connection with others.

As I listened to my friends, I noticed how their stories resonated with my own. We all faced challenges, yet we each found ways to cultivate gratitude amidst them. I felt a sense of solidarity, knowing that we were all navigating the complexities of life together. This gathering solidified my understanding that gratitude not only aids in individual healing but also strengthens our bonds with others.

Over time, I began to integrate gratitude into my daily life in more meaningful ways. I started expressing appreciation to those around me more openly. I made it a point to send thank-you notes to friends and family, acknowledging their impact on my life. I found that these small acts of gratitude deepened my relationships, creating a ripple effect of positivity.

One afternoon, I visited my grandmother, who had been feeling unwell. I brought along a simple bouquet of flowers, along with a heartfelt note expressing my love and appreciation for the wisdom she had shared throughout my life. As I watched her face light up, I felt an overwhelming sense of joy. In that moment, I realized that gratitude has a unique power to heal not only the giver but also the recipient. We both left that visit feeling uplifted, connected, and nourished by the simple act of appreciation.

As I continued my journey with gratitude, I also discovered the importance of self-compassion. I often struggled with feelings of inadequacy, especially during difficult times. However, I learned that gratitude could extend inward. I began to practice self-gratitude, acknowledging my efforts and progress. I wrote about the things I appreciated about myself—the resilience I had shown, the kindness I offered to others, and the courage it took to face my fears.

One evening, I sat down with my journal and reflected on my journey thus far. I wrote, "I am grateful for my strength, for my ability to rise after each fall, and for my willingness to learn from every experience." As I penned those words, I felt a shift within. I realized that self-gratitude was not about boasting; it was about honoring my journey and recognizing my worthiness. This practice became a vital aspect of my healing, allowing me to embrace myself with love and understanding.

The deeper I delved into gratitude, the more I began to notice its transformative power in my mindset. I started to see challenges not as obstacles but as opportunities for growth. One day, I faced a significant setback at work—a project I had invested countless hours into fell through unexpectedly. Initially, I felt a wave of frustration wash over me, but then I paused. I remembered my gratitude practice and asked myself, "What can I learn from this?"

As I reflected, I recognized that setbacks often pave the way for new opportunities. I felt grateful for the lessons learned throughout the process and for the chance to reassess my goals. I reached out to my colleagues for feedback, viewing this as a collaborative effort rather than a personal failure. This shift in perspective became a catalyst for growth, leading to new ideas and a renewed sense of purpose.

One evening, while reflecting on my gratitude journey, I felt inspired to create a gratitude jar. I decorated a simple jar with colorful paper and placed it on my desk, ready to fill it with moments of appreciation. Each time I experienced a moment of gratitude, I would write it down on a slip of paper and add it to the jar. Over time, the jar filled with notes—reminders of the beauty and abundance in my life.

As I looked at the jar, I felt a sense of joy swell within me. It became a tangible representation of my gratitude practice, a source of inspiration during challenging times. Whenever I faced moments of doubt or negativity, I would reach for the jar, pulling out random notes to remind myself of the goodness that surrounded me.

As the months passed, I continued to cultivate gratitude in various aspects of my life. I became more mindful of my thoughts and words, choosing to focus on the positive rather than getting caught up in negativity. I noticed how this shift not only improved my mood but also influenced those around me. Friends began to comment on my positive energy, and I realized that gratitude is contagious—it spreads like wildfire, igniting hope and joy in others.

One day, I decided to take my gratitude practice a step further by volunteering at a local shelter. I wanted to extend my appreciation for the life I had been given by giving back to others. As I served meals and connected with individuals facing difficulties, I felt a deep sense of fulfillment. The experience opened my eyes to the power of gratitude in action. I realized that by serving others, I could multiply the healing effects of gratitude, creating a ripple effect of kindness in the world.

Through these experiences, I discovered that gratitude is not simply a fleeting emotion; it is a powerful tool for healing and transformation. I learned that it nurtures resilience, allowing us to face challenges with an open heart. It fosters connections, reminding us of our shared humanity. And perhaps most importantly, it invites us to celebrate the beauty of life, even amidst the struggles.

As I reflect on my journey with gratitude, I feel a profound sense of appreciation for all that I have learned. I no longer view gratitude as a mere practice; it has become a way of life. I carry it with me, integrating it into my daily routine and interactions. Each morning, I express gratitude for the new day ahead. Each evening, I reflect on the moments that brought me joy. This simple shift in perspective has opened my heart and mind to the abundance that surrounds me.

In closing, I encourage you to explore the healing power of gratitude in your own life. Embrace it as a practice, a mindset, and a way of being. Allow it to guide you through challenges, nurturing your resilience and fostering connection. Remember that gratitude is not about denying pain or difficulty; it is about acknowledging the entirety of your experience and finding beauty within it. Together, let us celebrate the transformative power of gratitude and the profound healing it offers to our hearts and souls.

Prayers of Thanksgiving

There's a quiet magic in the simple act of saying thank you. I didn't always see it that way, though. For most of my life, I thought of gratitude as a polite formality, something nice to do, sure, but not something with any profound power. And then, during a particularly rough chapter of my life, I found myself turning to it in prayer. I wasn't sure what else to do. I had exhausted my energy, my options, and, if I'm being honest, my patience. So, I tried something different: I gave thanks for the things I still had. I started with the obvious—my health, my family, the roof over my head. And as I did, I felt something shift. It was subtle but undeniable. I'd stumbled into a new way of seeing life, a way that healed and uplifted me more than I could have ever imagined.

One of the first things I noticed when I began praying with gratitude was how my focus changed. In the past, my prayers had often been a running list of my troubles, my wants, my fears. But this time, it was different. I started by thanking the universe—or God, or whatever higher force was listening—for my little moments of peace. I thanked it for the crisp morning air, the warmth of my coffee cup, the way sunlight slanted through my window. I gave thanks for things that were usually background noise in my busy life, things I took for granted every day. And what I noticed was that my heart felt lighter, and my worries seemed to fade, even if just a little.

I remember one morning in particular. It was one of those days where nothing seemed to be going my way. I'd woken up late, spilled coffee on my shirt, and to top it off, I realized I'd completely forgotten an important deadline. Normally, I'd have let that day's mishaps sour my mood entirely. But I decided to take a moment to pray, to give thanks despite it all. I thanked God for the extra ten minutes of sleep, for the humor in my coffee mishap, and for the learning experience of the missed deadline. To my surprise, I felt my frustration ease. That day didn't magically become perfect, but it felt less like a disaster and more like a series of manageable blips. I discovered that by choosing gratitude, I was choosing resilience.

It wasn't just the small stuff, either. I found myself giving thanks for the hard lessons, the challenges, and even the losses. There was a particular experience that stands out to me—one that was difficult to talk about, let alone feel grateful for. I had just gone through a significant loss, the kind that leaves you hollow and aching. My instinct was to retreat, to shut myself off and hide from the world. But I knew that wouldn't bring peace. So, I tried something else. I thanked God for the time I'd had, for the memories I'd carry forward, and even for the pain, which reminded me just how deeply I could love. It wasn't easy. There were many tears shed, and I won't pretend it brought instant comfort. But over time, it helped me make peace with what had happened. My prayers of gratitude became a balm for my grief, a reminder that even in loss, there is something worth holding on to.

This journey of giving thanks didn't just change my outlook—it changed my relationships, too. I started noticing how often I took people for granted, assuming they'd always be there, expecting their support without a second thought. One evening, I sat down with this realization and prayed, offering gratitude for the people in my life. I thanked God for each friend, each family member, for their presence and their patience, even when I hadn't always reciprocated it. And something beautiful happened. I felt an urge to reach out to them, to let them know how much they meant to me. It wasn't an extravagant gesture, but it was heartfelt. I made a point to call, to send a quick message, to share my appreciation more openly. And what I noticed was that these connections deepened, becoming a source of strength and joy that I hadn't fully realized before.

My gratitude prayers also opened my eyes to the beauty of everyday moments. I realized that a day doesn't have to be filled with major victories or grand gestures to be meaningful. A peaceful morning, a shared laugh, a quiet evening with a good book—these became moments I cherished, moments I thanked God for in my quiet reflections. I learned to savor these small joys, to let them fill me up rather than waiting for some future happiness that might never come. There's a richness in ordinary life that I hadn't appreciated before, a beauty that comes from simply being present and grateful.

There was one particular evening that remains etched in my mind. I had just wrapped up a long, tiring day, and all I wanted was to sit down and rest. As I settled onto my couch, a wave of gratitude washed over me. I thanked God for that couch, for the roof over my head, for the food in my fridge. And as I sat there, immersed in this feeling, I realized how incredibly blessed I was. The world around me hadn't changed, but my heart had. I saw my life not as a series of tasks or achievements, but as a precious gift, filled with blessings both big and small.

Over time, I noticed that these prayers of thanksgiving began to shape my perspective in ways I hadn't expected. I started to see challenges as opportunities, setbacks as stepping stones, and even my struggles as part of a bigger plan. There was a period when I was working on a project that seemed to hit one roadblock after another. It felt like every time I made progress, something would push me two steps back. Frustration simmered, and I was ready to throw in the towel. But one night, as I was praying, I decided to thank God for the difficulties, for the patience and resilience they were teaching me. I won't lie—it felt strange to express gratitude for something that was causing me so much stress. But in doing so, I found a renewed sense of determination. I saw the obstacles not as signs to quit but as challenges to overcome. And, looking back, I can see how those tough moments strengthened me, how they taught me things I might never have learned otherwise.

Gratitude, I've found, is a choice. It's not always the easy one, and sometimes it feels almost impossible. But when I choose it, I feel a peace that goes beyond my circumstances. It's as if my gratitude connects me to something larger, reminding me that I am part of a beautiful, intricate tapestry. Even when life feels chaotic or painful, this sense of gratitude anchors me, helping me see beyond the immediate and trust in a greater purpose.

One of the most profound aspects of my journey with gratitude has been learning to be thankful for myself. I spent years being my harshest critic, quick to point out my flaws, slow to forgive my mistakes. But through my prayers, I began to shift this perspective. I started by thanking God for my body, for its strength and resilience. I thanked God for my mind, for its curiosity and its capacity to learn. I even thanked God for my mistakes, which taught me valuable lessons and brought me closer to the person I wanted to be. This practice wasn't easy—it's far simpler to extend kindness to others than to ourselves. But over time, I noticed a gentleness growing within me, a new appreciation for who I was, flaws and all.

These days, gratitude is woven into my life in ways that I never anticipated. It's there in the quiet moments of my morning, as I savor my first cup of coffee. It's there in my relationships, in the small acts of kindness I strive to show and receive. And it's there in my prayers, my heartfelt thanks for the life I've been given, for each breath, each opportunity to love and be loved.

In embracing gratitude, I've found a profound healing. It doesn't erase the pain or make everything perfect, but it offers a new way of seeing, a new way of being. Gratitude has transformed my mindset, helping me to focus not on what I lack but on the abundance already present in my life. It has taught me that peace isn't something I need to chase; it's something I can cultivate, moment by moment, through the simple act of saying thank you.

As I continue this journey, I know that gratitude will be my guide. I don't know what challenges or blessings lie ahead, but I do know that I will meet them with a thankful heart. And for that, I am endlessly grateful.

Shifting Focus from Lack to Abundance

I never imagined that a simple shift in perspective could completely transform my life, but that's exactly what happened when I discovered the healing power of gratitude. For years, I had been trapped in a mindset of lack, constantly focusing on what I didn't have and what was missing from my life. Little did I know that the key to unlocking abundance and joy was already within me, waiting to be discovered?

My journey began on what seemed like an ordinary Tuesday morning. I woke up feeling the familiar weight of dissatisfaction pressing down on my chest. As I went through my usual routine - brewing coffee, scrolling through social media, and getting ready for work - I couldn't shake the nagging feeling that something was missing. My job felt unfulfilling, my relationships seemed shallow, and my bank account was far from where I wanted it to be.

As I drove to work that day, stuck in traffic and stewing in my own frustration, I happened to turn on a podcast about gratitude. At first, I scoffed at the idea. How could simply being thankful change anything about my circumstances? But something about the speaker's words resonated with me, and I found myself listening intently.

The podcast host challenged listeners to start a gratitude practice, beginning with just three things each day. It seemed simple enough, so I decided to give it a try. That evening, I sat down with a notebook and pen, determined to find three things to be grateful for. To my surprise, once I started, I found it difficult to stop at just three. I wrote about the warm cup of tea I had enjoyed that morning, the kind smile from a stranger at the grocery store, and the comfortable bed I would soon sleep in.

As I continued this practice day after day, I began to notice subtle shifts in my perception. The world around me seemed brighter somehow, more vibrant. I started to appreciate the small moments that I had previously overlooked - the way sunlight filtered through leaves, the sound of laughter from children playing in the park, the aroma of freshly baked bread from the local bakery.

One particularly memorable moment came about a month into my gratitude practice. I was taking my usual walk in the park near my home when I suddenly stopped in my tracks, overwhelmed by a sense of wonder. The trees, which I had passed countless times before without a second glance, now seemed to pulse with life and energy. I could hear the symphony of birdsong, feel the gentle caress of the breeze on my skin, and smell the earthy scent of the forest floor. In that moment, I felt profoundly connected to everything around me, and a wave of gratitude washed over me so powerfully that tears sprang to my eyes.

This experience marked a turning point in my journey. I realized that gratitude wasn't just about listing things I was thankful for - it was a gateway to a whole new way of experiencing the world. I began to approach each day with a sense of curiosity and openness, eager to discover new reasons to be grateful.

As my gratitude practice deepened, I noticed changes in other areas of my life as well. At work, instead of focusing on the tasks I disliked or the colleagues who annoyed me, I started to appreciate the opportunities for growth and learning that my job provided. I found myself volunteering for new projects and taking on challenges that I would have previously avoided. To my surprise, this shift in attitude led to new opportunities and even a promotion.

In my relationships, I began to focus on the qualities I appreciated in my friends and family members, rather than dwelling on their flaws or the ways they disappointed me. This change in perspective not only deepened my existing relationships but also opened me up to forming new connections. I found myself striking up conversations with strangers and forming friendships with people I might have previously overlooked.

One of the most profound changes occurred in my relationship with myself. As I practiced gratitude, I began to appreciate my own qualities and accomplishments, rather than constantly comparing myself to others or focusing on my perceived shortcomings. I started treating myself with more kindness and compassion, which in turn allowed me to extend that same kindness to others.

However, my journey wasn't always smooth sailing. There were days when finding things to be grateful for felt like an insurmountable challenge. I remember one particularly difficult period when I lost my job unexpectedly. At first, I felt myself slipping back into old patterns of negative thinking and self-pity. But then I remembered my gratitude practice.

Even in the midst of uncertainty and fear, I forced myself to find things to be thankful for each day. I expressed gratitude for the severance package that would tide me over for a few months, for the support of friends who offered encouragement and job leads, and for the unexpected free time that allowed me to pursue interests I had long neglected.

To my amazement, this shift in focus completely changed my experience of unemployment. Instead of feeling like a victim of circumstance, I began to see this period as an opportunity for growth and self-discovery. I used my time to volunteer at a local community center, which not only gave me a sense of purpose but also led to valuable networking opportunities. I also rediscovered my passion for painting, spending hours lost in the creative process and feeling grateful for the ability to express myself through art.

When I eventually found a new job, it was in a field I had never considered before but which aligned perfectly with my values and interests. Looking back, I realized that if I hadn't lost my previous job and maintained a gratitude practice through that challenging time, I might never have discovered this new path.

As my gratitude practice continued to evolve, I began to explore other spiritual practices that complemented and deepened my sense of appreciation for life. I started meditating regularly, which helped me cultivate a greater sense of presence and awareness. This, in turn, allowed me to notice even more things to be grateful for in each moment.

I also discovered the power of expressing gratitude directly to others. I made it a point to tell people in my life what I appreciated about them, whether it was a coworker who always brought positive energy to team meetings or a neighbor who took the time to ask how I was doing. The reactions I received were heartwarming - people's faces would light up, and often they would share something they appreciated about me in return. These exchanges created a beautiful cycle of positivity and connection.

One particularly powerful experience came when I decided to write a letter of gratitude to my parents. Growing up, our relationship had been strained at times, and I had often focused on the ways I felt they had let me down or misunderstood me. But as I sat down to write, I found myself reflecting on all the sacrifices they had made for me, the values they had instilled, and the unconditional love they had always offered, even when I pushed them away.

Writing that letter was an emotional process, bringing up feelings of regret for the times I had taken them for granted, but also a deep sense of appreciation for the foundation they had given me. When I finally shared the letter with them, the conversation that followed was one of the most honest and healing exchanges we had ever had. It opened up a new chapter in our relationship, one based on mutual understanding and gratitude.

As my practice deepened, I began to notice that gratitude was not just changing my perception of the world, but it was actually attracting more positive experiences into my life. It was as if the universe was responding to my appreciation by providing even more to be grateful for. I found myself experiencing a series of synchronicities and "lucky" coincidences that seemed too perfect to be mere chance.

For example, shortly after I had expressed gratitude for the opportunity to travel more, a friend reached out with an unexpected invitation to join her on a trip to Bali - a place I had always dreamed of visiting but never thought I'd have the chance to see. During that trip, I had a profound spiritual experience while watching the sunrise from the top of a volcano. As I stood there, surrounded by breathtaking beauty, I felt an overwhelming sense of gratitude not just for that moment, but for every experience - good and bad - that had led me to that point in my life.

It was during this trip that I also discovered the concept of "radical gratitude" - the practice of finding things to be thankful for even in the most challenging or painful situations. This idea revolutionized my approach to difficulties in life. Instead of resisting or resenting obstacles, I began to ask myself, "What can I learn from this? What is this experience here to teach me?"

This shift was put to the test when I returned home and faced a health scare. Initial tests had come back with concerning results, and I was scheduled for further examinations. In the past, this kind of situation would have sent me into a spiral of fear and anxiety. But now, armed with my gratitude practice, I approached it differently.

I found myself feeling grateful for the early detection, for the advanced medical care available to me, and for the support of loved ones who rallied around me. I even found gratitude for the wake-up call this health scare provided, prompting me to prioritize my well-being and make necessary lifestyle changes.

When further tests eventually came back clear, my relief was profound, but so was my appreciation for the entire experience. It had shown me the strength of my support network, the resilience of my spirit, and the power of maintaining a positive outlook even in the face of uncertainty.

As my journey with gratitude continued, I began to see it as more than just a personal practice - it became a lens through which I viewed the world and a tool for creating positive change. I started to look for ways to spread gratitude in my community. I organized gratitude circles where people could come together to share what they were thankful for and support each other in maintaining a positive mindset.

I also initiated a "Gratitude Project" at my workplace, encouraging colleagues to express appreciation for each other's contributions. The impact was remarkable - morale improved, collaboration increased, and the overall atmosphere became more positive and supportive.

Through these experiences, I came to understand that gratitude is not just a passive feeling, but an active force that can transform individuals, relationships, and even entire communities. It has the power to bridge divides, heal wounds, and create connections where none existed before.

As I reflect on my journey from a mindset of lack to one of abundance, I'm amazed at how far I've come. The person I am today - more joyful, more resilient, more connected - sometimes feels worlds apart from the dissatisfied, anxious individual I used to be. Yet I know that transformation didn't happen overnight. It was the result of consistent practice, of choosing gratitude day after day, even (and especially) when it wasn't easy.

I've learned that gratitude is not about denying the challenges or difficulties in life. It's not about forcing positivity or pretending everything is perfect. Rather, it's about expanding our perception to include all aspects of our experience - the good and the bad, the easy and the difficult. It's about recognizing that even in our darkest moments, there is always something to be grateful for, even if it's just the breath in our lungs or the beating of our hearts.

Moreover, I've discovered that gratitude is not a destination but an ongoing journey. There are still days when I struggle, when old patterns of negative thinking try to reassert themselves. But now I have tools to combat these tendencies. I know that no matter how I'm feeling, I can always return to gratitude as my anchor, my compass, my way back to center.

If you're reading this and feeling skeptical, as I once was, about the power of gratitude to transform your life, I encourage you to give it a try. Start small - find three things to be grateful for each day. Write them down, say them out loud, or simply hold them in your heart. Be patient with yourself and with the process. Like any skill, cultivating gratitude takes practice.

Remember that gratitude is not about comparing your life to others or feeling guilty for what you have. It's about recognizing and appreciating the abundance that already exists in your life, no matter your circumstances. It's about shifting your focus from what's wrong to what's right, from what's missing to what's present.

As you embark on or continue your own gratitude journey, know that you're not just changing your own life - you're contributing to a larger shift in consciousness. Every time you choose gratitude over complaint, appreciation over criticism, you're sending ripples of positivity out into the world.

In a world that often seems dominated by negativity and division, gratitude offers a powerful antidote. It reminds us of our shared humanity, our interconnectedness, and the fundamental goodness that exists in life. It opens our hearts, expands our perspective, and allows us to tap into the limitless abundance of the universe.

So I invite you to join me in this gratitude revolution. Let's shift our focus from lack to abundance, from fear to love, from separation to connection. Let's harness the healing power of gratitude to transform not just our own lives, but the world around us. For in the end, a life lived in gratitude is a life lived fully, deeply, and joyfully - and that, perhaps, is the greatest gift we can give to ourselves and to the world.

Gratitude as a Daily Practice

Gratitude has woven itself into the very fabric of my daily life, becoming more than just a fleeting emotion; it has transformed into a daily practice that nourishes my spirit and reshapes my mindset. I still vividly remember the moment when I realized the profound impact gratitude could have on my well-being. It was a crisp autumn morning, and I sat on my porch, sipping coffee while watching the leaves dance in the breeze. As I took in the beauty of the world around me, I felt a gentle nudge from within, urging me to acknowledge the blessings in my life.

At first, I hesitated. I had always considered gratitude an important virtue but rarely made time to practice it intentionally. I often found myself caught up in the whirlwind of daily responsibilities, focusing more on what I lacked than what I had. That morning, however, something shifted. I picked up my journal, opened it to a fresh page, and wrote down three things I was grateful for. The act felt simple, almost trivial, yet it sparked a flicker of warmth in my heart.

I wrote about the gentle sunlight that kissed my skin, the aroma of freshly brewed coffee, and the laughter of my children echoing from inside the house. As I reflected on each item, I felt a wave of appreciation wash over me. It was as if a curtain had lifted, revealing the beauty of ordinary moments that I had overlooked in my haste. That day marked the beginning of my journey into gratitude as a daily practice.

The next morning, I repeated the exercise. This time, I focused on different aspects of my life. I found myself writing about the support of my partner, the health of my loved ones, and the joy of a good book. Each entry became a small celebration of life's richness. I started to notice how these moments of reflection created a ripple effect throughout my day. I became more aware of my surroundings, noticing the laughter of children playing in the park, the kindness of a stranger, and even the taste of my food. Gratitude began to color my experiences in vibrant hues, reminding me that beauty exists even amidst the mundane.

One day, while grappling with a particularly stressful week at work, I felt the weight of anxiety pressing down on me. I had a project deadline looming, and it consumed my thoughts. I sat at my desk, overwhelmed by the tasks ahead, when I decided to take a break and practice gratitude. I closed my eyes, took a deep breath, and recounted the things I appreciated. I thought about the support of my colleagues, the opportunity to pursue work I was passionate about, and even the coffee that fueled my late nights.

As I reflected, I felt my anxiety begin to dissipate. I realized that while challenges may arise, I had the tools and resources to navigate them. Gratitude shifted my focus from what I lacked to what I had—skills, support, and the ability to adapt. This newfound perspective empowered me to tackle my tasks with renewed energy.

As my gratitude practice deepened, I began to explore different ways to incorporate it into my daily routine. I started keeping a gratitude jar, a simple glass container filled with notes of appreciation. Each evening, I would write down a moment or experience that brought me joy and fold it up before placing it in the jar. Over time, the jar filled with colorful slips of paper, each one a testament to the beauty I had encountered. On days when I felt overwhelmed, I would reach for the jar and read through the notes, reminding myself of the abundance in my life.

One evening, I invited my family to join me in this practice. We gathered around the dining table, lit a few candles, and shared our moments of gratitude. The conversation flowed effortlessly as we laughed and reminisced about our favorite memories. I listened as my children expressed their appreciation for simple joys—a sunny day at the park, a delicious meal, and each other's companionship. That night, I felt a profound sense of connection; gratitude had transformed our family dinner into a celebration of love and togetherness.

As the months rolled on, I began to notice how gratitude impacted my relationships. I became more intentional about expressing appreciation to those around me. Instead of taking my partner's support for granted, I made it a point to voice my gratitude regularly. I would leave little notes around the house—on the bathroom mirror, in his lunch, or tucked into his favorite book. The simple act of acknowledging his presence and support deepened our bond. Each time he found one of my notes, I could see the joy in his eyes; it was a reminder that gratitude is a language of love.

During this time, I also faced personal challenges. A close friend of mine went through a difficult period, battling illness. I felt helpless, wanting to support her but unsure how to make a meaningful impact. I turned to gratitude, reflecting on the moments we had shared—our late-night talks, our laughter, and the adventures we embarked on together. Inspired, I decided to send her a care package filled with her favorite snacks, a heartfelt letter, and a small journal for her to jot down her thoughts.

In my letter, I expressed my gratitude for her friendship and the light she brought into my life. I shared how her strength inspired me, even during her toughest days. When she received the package, she called me, her voice filled with emotion. She thanked me for being there and for reminding her of the love that surrounded her. In that moment, I realized that gratitude not only uplifts our spirits but also has the power to heal connections.

One particularly challenging week, I faced my own health scare. The anxiety spiraled within me as I awaited test results, my mind racing with worst-case scenarios. I felt the familiar grip of fear tightening around my chest, but I knew I had to ground myself. I turned to my gratitude practice, writing down everything I appreciated that day. I focused on the small things—my cozy blanket, the sound of raindrops tapping against the window, and the support of my loved ones.

As I wrote, I felt a shift within me. Gratitude became my refuge, a place to retreat when fear threatened to overwhelm me. I realized that regardless of the outcome of my health concerns, I had the power to choose how I responded. I could embrace the uncertainty with grace and appreciation for the present moment. This insight became a cornerstone of my healing journey, teaching me that gratitude is a powerful antidote to fear.

In time, I learned to extend my gratitude practice beyond my personal life. I began volunteering at a local community center, where I helped organize events for families in need. Each week, I witnessed the resilience of those I served, and I felt an overwhelming sense of gratitude for the opportunity to contribute. I learned that giving back not only nourished my spirit but also deepened my understanding of gratitude's role in fostering community.

During one particular event, I met a single mother who shared her story of struggle and resilience. She spoke of the challenges she faced while raising her children alone. As she shared, I felt a profound sense of empathy. I realized that gratitude isn't just about acknowledging our own blessings; it's about recognizing the struggles and triumphs of others. I expressed my appreciation for her strength, and we connected on a deeper level.

As I continued my volunteer work, I often found myself reflecting on the lessons I learned from those I served. Each interaction became an opportunity for growth, teaching me that gratitude is a two-way street. I learned to appreciate not only the help I offered but also the lessons I received from others. This exchange of gratitude created a sense of unity, reminding me that we are all interconnected.

Months turned into years, and my gratitude practice became a natural part of my daily routine. I began each morning by sipping my coffee quietly, reflecting on what I was thankful for before diving into the day's tasks. I cherished those moments of stillness, allowing gratitude to set a positive tone for the day ahead. I found that when I started my day with appreciation, I approached challenges with a clearer mind and an open heart.

One evening, I attended a workshop on mindfulness and self-care. The facilitator invited us to share our experiences with gratitude. As I listened to others speak, I felt a wave of inspiration wash over me. Each person shared how gratitude had transformed their lives, and I realized that I was part of a larger movement—a community of individuals committed to fostering positivity and healing.

After the workshop, I reflected on my journey. I recognized that gratitude had not only changed my mindset but also shaped my identity. I had grown into a person who actively sought out moments of appreciation, who understood the importance of expressing gratitude to others, and who embraced the beauty of life's imperfections. I felt empowered by the realization that gratitude is a practice, a choice I could make every day.

As I continued to embrace gratitude, I became more aware of its transformative power in the face of adversity. I encountered challenges that tested my resilience, but I found comfort in my gratitude practice. When life felt overwhelming, I turned to my journal, pouring my thoughts onto the pages and finding solace in the act of reflection. I learned that gratitude doesn't erase pain; it coexists with it, offering a gentle reminder of hope.

One day, I faced a significant setback in my career. A project I had poured my heart into was shelved, leaving me feeling disheartened and uncertain about my future. In that moment, I felt the familiar urge to spiral into negativity. Instead, I paused and turned to my gratitude practice. I wrote down the lessons I had learned, the skills I had developed, and the support I had received from colleagues. I realized that this setback was not the end but rather an opportunity for growth and exploration.

As I navigated through the uncertainty, I found strength in my gratitude practice. I began to seek out new opportunities, networking with others and exploring different paths. Each step I took was fueled by the understanding that gratitude would guide me through the unknown. I learned to embrace change with an open heart, trusting that whatever came next would unfold in its own time.

As time passed, I began to notice how gratitude had become a lens through which I viewed the world. I approached life with a sense of curiosity, eager to uncover the beauty in everyday moments. I found joy in the simplest of things—a warm cup of tea, a heartfelt conversation with a friend, or the sound of laughter filling my home. Gratitude transformed my perception, allowing me to see the richness of life even amidst challenges.

In closing, I encourage you to cultivate gratitude as a daily practice. Embrace it as a tool for healing, growth, and connection. Allow it to guide you through life's ups and downs, reminding you of the beauty that exists in the world. Each day presents an opportunity to discover something new to be grateful for, and in doing so, you can transform your mindset and enrich your life. Together, let us celebrate the power of gratitude and the profound healing it brings to our hearts and souls.

The Ripple Effect of a Grateful Heart

I'll never forget the moment I first truly felt the power of gratitude. It was one of those ordinary days, the kind that blends into countless others, but something remarkable happened. I had just finished a long day of work, feeling drained and wrapped up in my usual routine of unwinding with a book. Out of nowhere, an overwhelming sense of gratitude hit me like a wave. I was suddenly aware of the warmth of my home, the quiet in the air, and the comfort of simply being. I felt a deep sense of peace I couldn't explain, as if I had tapped into some hidden reservoir of energy and calm within myself. That moment ignited something, a spark that showed me how life-changing gratitude could be.

As I began to explore this feeling more intentionally, I noticed subtle but meaningful shifts in my everyday interactions. I found myself smiling more, engaging with people in a way that felt more genuine. Whether I was thanking the barista for my coffee, waving at a neighbor, or calling a friend to check in, I felt that my small gestures of gratitude made a difference. It was as though the gratitude I was carrying inside of me was spreading outwards, touching the lives of those around me. And the beautiful thing was, they responded. My smiles were met with smiles; my gestures of kindness seemed to inspire kindness in return. It felt like dropping a stone into a still pond and watching the ripples extend far beyond the point of impact. Little did I know then that these small acts of gratitude would create a ripple effect that would transform my life?

One of the most significant changes I noticed as I nurtured a grateful heart was in my closest relationships. There was a time when I had been more prone to focus on what was missing—wishing friends and family would be more attentive or supportive in ways I felt were lacking. But with gratitude at the center of my mindset, I began to see everything I had overlooked before. I started to appreciate the small gestures—a text to check in, a quick coffee date, a shared laugh over a silly memory. My gratitude helped me recognize that love often shows up in these everyday moments, and when I started to focus on these small blessings, I found myself feeling closer to my loved ones than ever before.

There was one particular experience with a friend that sticks out. We had drifted apart over the years, mainly due to busy schedules and the natural ebb and flow of life. We'd text sporadically, but something felt missing. One day, I decided to reach out with a heartfelt message, just letting her know how much I appreciated her and all the moments we'd shared, no matter how long ago they were. I wasn't expecting much; I just felt compelled to say it. To my surprise, she replied almost immediately, sharing how she'd felt the same way and had been hesitant to reach out. That simple expression of gratitude opened a door we hadn't even realized was closed. We reconnected in a way that felt fresh and real, and to this day, that friendship remains a source of strength and joy. That experience taught me how a grateful heart can revive relationships that might otherwise fade into the background.

Even in professional settings, I saw how my gratitude had a ripple effect. I made a point to express appreciation to my colleagues for their hard work and support, a habit I hadn't previously thought much about. A quick thank-you email after a meeting or a sincere compliment during a hectic day seemed to lift not just my mood but everyone's. I noticed that when I took a moment to genuinely acknowledge others, it set a tone that felt more collaborative and supportive. People began reciprocating, and soon, we had a team culture where gratitude was part of our day-to-day. What started as a small effort on my part had blossomed into something that made the workplace a little more positive for everyone. It was humbling to see that something as simple as gratitude could inspire others and create a more uplifting environment.

The most profound effect of all, though, was within myself. Living with gratitude allowed me to experience a shift in my inner dialogue. I stopped being so hard on myself, and rather than focusing on my mistakes or perceived shortcomings, I learned to appreciate my growth. I thanked myself for the courage to try new things, for the resilience I'd shown during difficult times, and for the patience to keep going even when the path felt unclear. This kindness toward myself was new, and it wasn't easy at first. I had to unlearn years of self-criticism and perfectionism, but little by little, gratitude helped me heal. I realized that gratitude, when directed inward, nurtures self-compassion, and that self-compassion opens doors to self-love and acceptance in ways I hadn't thought possible.

There was a time when I faced a particularly tough setback, one that had me questioning my choices and even my self-worth. In the past, I would have spiraled into a cycle of self-doubt and frustration, but this time, I tried something different. I took a deep breath and said a prayer of thanks—not because I felt grateful for the setback, but because I trusted that it would teach me something valuable. I thanked the experience for the resilience it would build, for the insight it might eventually provide, and for the strength it would take for me to overcome it. In that moment, I felt a sense of peace that I hadn't known before. The gratitude didn't erase the disappointment, but it softened the blow and allowed me to move forward with a sense of purpose rather than defeat.

As I continued to live with a grateful heart, I noticed how even strangers responded differently to me. I'd strike up conversations in line at the grocery store, thank the cashier with genuine warmth, or offer a compliment to someone in passing. More often than not, people would smile, sometimes even stop to chat or share a bit of their day. It was as if gratitude had made me more open to connection, and that openness attracted connection in return. Each encounter reminded me of how interconnected we all are, and how a single, small gesture can brighten someone's day in ways we might never know. I realized that gratitude doesn't just improve our own lives; it ripples outward, touching those around us in unexpected and beautiful ways.

I remember one day in particular when I was at a coffee shop, waiting in line behind a woman who looked like she was having a rough day. She seemed tired, maybe even a bit sad, and I could sense a heaviness around her. When it was her turn, I quietly offered to buy her coffee, telling her it was a small act of kindness that had brightened my own day. She looked at me with a mixture of surprise and relief, as if she hadn't expected anyone to notice her struggles. We chatted briefly, and she thanked me with a smile that felt so genuine, it left me feeling as uplifted as she did. That experience reminded me that gratitude isn't just about saying thank you; it's about spreading kindness, one small action at a time.

Looking back, I can see that gratitude has shaped my life in ways I never could have planned. It's transformed my relationships, deepened my connections, and given me a renewed appreciation for life's simplest joys. It's allowed me to see beyond the superficial, to find beauty in the mundane, and to recognize that each day is a gift. Gratitude has been a guiding light through my darkest moments, reminding me that even in times of struggle, there is something to be thankful for. And in times of joy, it's shown me how to savor each moment, to let it fill me up in ways that last.

Living with a grateful heart has taught me that the real magic of gratitude lies in its ability to multiply. The more I practice it, the more it grows, touching the lives of those around me and, in turn, deepening my own sense of fulfillment. It's a reminder that no matter where we are or what we're going through, we can choose gratitude, and in choosing gratitude, we open ourselves to endless possibilities for connection, growth, and joy. In the end, a grateful heart doesn't just change our perspective; it transforms our lives, and through us, the lives of others. And that, I believe, is the true power of gratitude—its endless, beautiful ripple effect.

THE INTERPLAY OF BODY, MIND, AND SPIRIT: HOLISTIC HEALING THROUGH FAITH

Understanding Holistic Healing

I never imagined that a devastating car accident would become the catalyst for my journey into holistic healing, but life has a way of surprising us with its most profound lessons in the most unexpected moments. As I lay in the hospital bed, my body broken and my spirit crushed, I couldn't foresee the transformative path that lay ahead. Little did I know that this moment of darkness would lead me to discover the intricate interplay of body, mind, and spirit, and the powerful role faith would play in my healing journey?

The accident had left me with multiple fractures, internal injuries, and a concussion that clouded my thoughts. The road to recovery seemed impossibly long, and the constant pain was a stark reminder of how fragile our physical existence can be. Traditional medical treatments were necessary, of course, but as the days turned into weeks, I began to feel that something was missing in my healing process.

It was during one particularly challenging night, when sleep eluded me and pain seemed to be my only companion that I experienced what I can only describe as a moment of divine intervention. As I lay there, feeling utterly hopeless, I suddenly felt a warm, comforting presence envelop me. It wasn't a physical sensation, but rather an overwhelming sense of peace and love that seemed to come from both within and without.

In that moment, I heard a gentle voice - not with my ears, but somewhere deep in my consciousness - saying, "Healing is more than mending bones. It's about restoring wholeness to your entire being." This experience, brief as it was, planted a seed in my mind and heart. It sparked a curiosity about the nature of healing and a desire to explore beyond the confines of traditional medicine.

As soon as I was able, I began researching alternative healing modalities and holistic approaches to wellness. I devoured books on energy healing, mindfulness, and the connection between spiritual well-being and physical health. The more I learned, the more I realized that true healing involves a delicate balance of caring for the body, nurturing the mind, and nourishing the spirit.

My first practical step into holistic healing came in the form of meditation. Still confined to my hospital bed, I started with simple breathing exercises. At first, it was frustrating. My mind would wander, or I'd become distracted by pain or discomfort. But I persevered, gradually increasing the duration of my practice.

To my surprise, I began to notice subtle changes. The constant chatter in my mind started to quiet down, and I found moments of peace amidst the chaos of my recovery. More importantly, I began to develop a deeper awareness of my body. Instead of seeing it as a broken vessel that had failed me, I started to appreciate its incredible capacity for healing.

As I continued to explore meditation, I also began to reconnect with my faith. I had always considered myself spiritual, but my beliefs had been more of a background presence in my life rather than an active force. Now, in the face of this life-altering experience, I found myself turning to prayer with a new sense of earnestness and openness.

My prayers weren't just requests for physical healing, though that was certainly part of it. Instead, I found myself engaging in heartfelt conversations with a higher power, expressing gratitude for the smallest improvements, seeking guidance, and finding comfort in the belief that there was a greater purpose to my suffering.

This rekindled faith became a powerful force in my healing journey. It provided me with hope when medical prognoses seemed bleak, and it gave me the strength to push through grueling physical therapy sessions. But more than that, it opened my eyes to the spiritual dimension of healing - the idea that true wellness extends beyond the physical realm.

As my physical condition improved enough for me to leave the hospital, I was determined to continue exploring holistic healing modalities. I sought out a naturopathic doctor who took a comprehensive approach to health, considering not just my physical symptoms but also my emotional state, stress levels, and spiritual well-being.

Under her guidance, I began to make significant changes to my lifestyle. I overhauled my diet, replacing processed foods with nutrient-dense, whole foods. I learned about the healing properties of various herbs and started incorporating them into my daily routine. I also began practicing yoga, which not only helped with my physical rehabilitation but also deepened my mind-body connection.

One particularly transformative experience came during a restorative yoga session. As I held a gentle heart-opening pose, I suddenly felt an overwhelming surge of emotion. Tears began to flow, and I realized I was releasing pent-up fear, anger, and grief related to the accident. This emotional release felt just as healing as any physical therapy session I had undergone.

This experience highlighted for me the intricate connection between our emotional state and our physical health. I began to pay more attention to my emotions, acknowledging and processing them rather than suppressing them as I had often done in the past. I started journaling regularly, finding that the act of putting my thoughts and feelings on paper was incredibly cathartic.

As I delved deeper into holistic healing, I also became fascinated by the concept of energy healing. I was initially skeptical, but my curiosity led me to try a Reiki session. The practitioner explained that Reiki involves channeling universal life energy to promote healing and balance in the body.

During the session, as I lay on the treatment table with the practitioner's hands hovering over various parts of my body, I experienced sensations I couldn't explain - waves of warmth, tingling, and at times, a feeling of energy moving through me. But the most profound effect came after the session. I felt an incredible sense of calm and well-being that lasted for days.

This experience piqued my interest in the unseen energetic aspects of our being. I began to explore other energy healing modalities and even took courses to learn how to work with energy myself. As I practiced these techniques, I started to perceive the subtle energy field around my body and developed a greater sensitivity to the energetic imbalances that can manifest as physical or emotional issues.

Throughout this journey, my faith continued to deepen and evolve. I came to see spirituality not as a separate aspect of life, but as the thread that weaves together all aspects of our being. My prayers became more meditative, and I often found myself in a state of contemplative awareness, feeling deeply connected to something greater than myself.

This spiritual awareness began to infuse every aspect of my life. I started to see everyday activities as opportunities for mindfulness and connection with the divine. Something as simple as preparing a meal became a sacred act when done with intention and gratitude. My morning walk in nature became a moving meditation, each step a prayer of thanks for my recovering body and the beauty of the world around me.

As my healing progressed, I also became acutely aware of the power of community in the healing process. I joined a support group for accident survivors and found immense comfort in sharing my experiences and listening to others' stories. The sense of connection and understanding I found there was profoundly healing.

Inspired by this, I started a weekly gathering in my home, inviting friends and neighbors to join me for meditation and discussions about holistic health and spirituality. These gatherings became a source of joy and support, not just for me but for everyone involved. We shared knowledge, practiced healing techniques together, and celebrated each other's progress and insights.

One particularly memorable evening, we decided to hold a group healing ceremony. We created a sacred space in my living room, lit candles, and took turns lying in the center of our circle while the others sent healing energy and prayers. The atmosphere was charged with love and positive intention. As I lay there, surrounded by the caring energy of the group, I felt a profound shift within me. It was as if the last lingering shadows of trauma from the accident were finally being released.

This experience underscored for me the power of collective intention and the importance of community in the healing process. It showed me that while individual practices are crucial, there's something uniquely powerful about coming together with others in a spirit of healing and support.

As my journey continued, I began to notice synchronicities and what some might call miracles in my life. Small coincidences that seemed to guide me towards the next step in my healing, unexpected encounters with people who had just the right knowledge or experience to share, and moments of insight that seemed to come from a higher source.

One such moment occurred during a solitary retreat I took in nature. I had gone to a nearby forest for a weekend of reflection and meditation. On the second day, as I sat by a stream in silent contemplation, I had a vivid inner vision. I saw my body not as a solid form, but as a complex network of energy pathways. I could perceive how these pathways connected my physical body with my thoughts, emotions, and what I can only describe as my soul.

In that moment, I understood on a deep level that true healing isn't about fixing separate parts of ourselves, but about restoring harmony and flow to our entire being. I saw how an imbalance in one area - be it physical, mental, emotional, or spiritual - could affect all other aspects of our health.

This vision profoundly impacted my approach to healing. I began to see each challenge - whether it was residual pain from the accident, emotional upheaval, or spiritual questioning - as an opportunity to restore balance to my whole self. Instead of just treating symptoms, I started asking myself what each issue might be trying to teach me about my overall well-being.

As I integrated this holistic understanding into my life, I found myself naturally drawn to share my experiences with others. I started a blog where I wrote about my healing journey, offering insights and practical tips for others interested in holistic health. To my surprise, the blog gained a following, and I began receiving messages from people all over the world who were inspired by my story.

This unexpected turn led me to pursue formal training in holistic health coaching. I wanted to deepen my knowledge and develop the skills to guide others on their healing journeys. The training was intense but incredibly rewarding. It expanded my understanding of nutrition, stress management, and the myriad factors that influence our health.

As I began working with clients, I was continually amazed by the body's innate wisdom and capacity for healing. I saw how small changes in diet, lifestyle, and mindset could lead to profound transformations. But more than anything, I was struck by the importance of addressing the spiritual aspect of health.

Many of my clients came to me focused solely on physical symptoms, but as we worked together, they often discovered that their health issues were connected to deeper emotional or spiritual imbalances. Helping them reconnect with their own inner wisdom and spiritual beliefs, whatever form that took for them, was often the key to unlocking their healing potential.

One client's story particularly stands out. Sarah came to me struggling with chronic fatigue and recurrent infections. We worked on improving her diet and sleep habits, but the real breakthrough came when we explored the emotional roots of her exhaustion. Through guided meditations and journaling exercises, Sarah realized she had been suppressing her true passions and living a life that wasn't aligned with her values.

As Sarah began to make changes to live more authentically and pursue her dreams, her energy levels improved dramatically, and her health issues began to resolve. This experience was a powerful reminder of how our physical health is intimately connected to our emotional well-being and our sense of purpose and meaning in life.

Looking back on my journey, from the dark days following the accident to where I am now, I'm filled with awe and gratitude. What began as a personal quest for healing has blossomed into a life purpose. I've learned that healing is not a destination but an ongoing journey of growth, self-discovery, and connection with something greater than ourselves.

I've come to see that true holistic healing is about more than just integrating different treatment modalities. It's about recognizing the fundamental interconnectedness of all aspects of our being - body, mind, and spirit. It's about honoring the wisdom of our bodies, cultivating a positive and resilient mindset, and nurturing our spiritual connection.

Moreover, I've discovered that faith - whether in a higher power, in the innate wisdom of our bodies, or in the fundamental goodness of life - is a powerful catalyst for healing. It provides hope when the path seems dark, strength when we feel weak, and a sense of purpose that can carry us through the most challenging times.

As I continue on this path, I remain endlessly fascinated by the mysteries of healing and the incredible resilience of the human spirit. Each day brings new insights, challenges, and opportunities for growth. And while I may not have all the answers, I'm grateful for the journey and for the opportunity to share what I've learned with others.

To anyone reading this who may be on their own healing journey, I offer this encouragement: Trust in the process. Listen to your body, honor your emotions, and nourish your spirit. Seek out knowledge and support, but also trust your own inner wisdom. Remember that you are not broken, but a complex, miraculous being with an innate capacity for healing and growth.

And above all, have faith - in yourself, in the process of life, and in the interconnected web of existence of which we are all a part. For it is in this faith, this trust in something greater than ourselves, that we often find our greatest strength and our deepest healing.

The Role of Prayer in Physical Healing

Prayer has woven itself into the tapestry of my life, often serving as a lifeline during moments of physical distress. I still remember the first time I truly understood the profound role prayer could play in healing. It was a chilly evening, and I sat curled up on the couch, nursing a relentless headache that seemed to throb in time with my pulse. I had tried everything —over-the-counter pain relievers, herbal teas, even a cold compress—but nothing seemed to work. Frustration built within me, and in that moment of desperation, I decided to turn to prayer.

I closed my eyes and took a deep breath, letting the worries of the day melt away. I focused on the pain that radiated through my head, acknowledging it without judgment. "Please," I whispered, "help me find relief." As I voiced my concerns, something shifted within me. I felt a wave of calm wash over me, as if a warm light enveloped my body. In that moment, I realized prayer wasn't just about asking for help; it was about opening my heart to receive it.

Over the following days, I began to incorporate prayer into my daily routine. Each morning, I would set aside a few moments to connect with my inner self, expressing gratitude for the day ahead and asking for strength and healing. I found a sense of comfort in this practice, a gentle reminder that I was not alone in my struggles. I prayed not only for my physical ailments but also for the emotional and spiritual aspects of my life. I understood that healing required a holistic approach, one that recognized the interplay of body, mind, and spirit.

One afternoon, I found myself grappling with a more significant health challenge. I had been experiencing persistent fatigue, a heaviness that seemed to seep into every aspect of my life. I consulted with doctors, underwent tests, and tried various remedies, but nothing appeared to provide a lasting solution. The fatigue weighed heavily on my spirit, and I felt as though I was living in a fog. In my moments of despair, I turned to prayer, seeking clarity and guidance.

As I prayed, I envisioned my body as a vessel, one that needed nurturing and care. I pictured each organ, each muscle, and each cell, thanking them for their hard work and resilience. I asked for healing not just for my physical body but also for my spirit, which felt battered and worn. I learned to listen during these moments of prayer, tuning in to the whispers of my intuition. I began to sense that my body was trying to communicate something to me—that it was time to slow down, to rest, and to reevaluate my lifestyle choices.

During this period, I made a conscious effort to incorporate more mindfulness into my daily routine. I started practicing meditation alongside my prayers, allowing myself to sit in stillness and simply be. I would close my eyes and focus on my breath, envisioning each inhale bringing in healing energy and each exhale releasing tension and negativity. This practice deepened my connection to prayer, transforming it into a dialogue between my body, mind, and spirit.

One evening, as I sat in meditation, I felt a surge of energy coursing through me. It was as if my body was awakening from a deep slumber, and in that moment, I understood that healing is not always a linear path. Sometimes, it requires patience and trust. I remembered a time when I had felt similar sensations during prayer. I had been struggling with anxiety, a constant companion that shadowed my every move. As I prayed, I recalled the moments when I felt light and free. I vowed to return to that state, to trust in the process of healing.

As my journey continued, I began to explore the connection between physical healing and prayer more deeply. I sought out communities where prayer was a collective experience. I participated in group prayer sessions, sharing my struggles and listening to the stories of others. Each gathering felt like a sacred space, a refuge where we could support one another in our healing journeys. I found strength in the collective energy of these gatherings, a reminder that we are all interconnected in our struggles and triumphs.

One particular evening, I attended a prayer circle focused on healing. As we gathered in a circle, the energy in the room felt palpable. We each shared our intentions, voicing the challenges we faced. When it was my turn, I spoke candidly about my fatigue and the toll it had taken on my spirit. As I shared, I felt a weight lift off my shoulders. The act of voicing my struggles felt cathartic, and I sensed the support of the group enveloping me like a warm blanket.

After our sharing, we entered into a period of silent prayer. We focused our intentions on healing, envisioning light and love surrounding each person in the circle. I closed my eyes and pictured myself bathed in radiant energy, feeling the warmth seep into every cell of my body. In that moment, I understood the power of collective prayer. It was as if a wave of healing energy flowed through us all, transcending our individual struggles and connecting us in a profound way.

As the weeks turned into months, I began to notice subtle shifts in my physical well-being. I still experienced fatigue, but it no longer consumed me. I learned to listen to my body, honoring its needs and responding with self-care. I explored nutrition, incorporating more whole foods and nourishing meals into my diet. I found joy in cooking, creating dishes that celebrated the vibrancy of life. Each meal became an offering, a way to honor my body and show gratitude for the healing journey I was on.

Prayer remained a cornerstone of my healing process. I began to visualize my body as a garden, one that required tending and care. I would close my eyes and imagine the seeds of healing being planted, nourished by my prayers and intentions. I pictured vibrant flowers blooming, each one a representation of the progress I was making. This visualization practice infused my prayers with intention, transforming them into a powerful tool for healing.

I also explored different forms of prayer, experimenting with what resonated with me. I found solace in writing prayers in my journal, pouring my heart onto the pages. Each entry became a sacred dialogue between me and the universe, a way to articulate my hopes, fears, and desires. I discovered that writing allowed me to process my emotions in a way that felt authentic and empowering.

One evening, I decided to write a prayer of gratitude for my body. I reflected on the countless ways it supported me each day, from the strength in my legs that carried me on walks to the soothing rhythm of my heartbeat. As I penned my words, I felt a wave of appreciation wash over me. I realized that prayer could be an offering of thanks, a way to honor the journey I was on, even in the face of challenges.

As I continued to deepen my spiritual practice, I encountered moments of doubt and uncertainty. There were days when fatigue would return, casting a shadow over my spirit. In those moments, I turned to prayer, asking for guidance and clarity. I reminded myself that healing is not always a linear path; it ebbs and flows like the tides. I learned to embrace the uncertainty, trusting that my prayers would guide me toward the light.

One afternoon, I found myself sitting in a park, surrounded by the beauty of nature. I took a deep breath and closed my eyes, allowing the sounds of birds chirping and leaves rustling to wash over me. In that serene moment, I offered a prayer of surrender. I released my need for control, allowing myself to simply be. I felt a deep sense of peace enveloping me, a reminder that I was part of something greater.

As my healing journey progressed, I began to notice the ripple effects of prayer in my relationships. I became more present with my loved ones, actively listening and supporting them in their struggles. I realized that prayer extends beyond the self; it connects us to one another. I started to invite my family into my prayer practice, encouraging them to express their intentions and share their experiences. Together, we created a sacred space for healing and connection.

One evening, as we gathered around the dinner table, I asked everyone to share their intentions for the week. We took turns voicing our hopes and challenges, and I felt a sense of unity enveloping us. After sharing, we held hands and offered a collective prayer, sending our intentions out into the universe. In that moment, I understood that prayer not only nurtured our individual journeys but also strengthened the bonds of our family.

As I continued to explore the role of prayer in physical healing, I stumbled upon the concept of energy healing. Intrigued, I began to learn about practices such as Reiki and acupuncture. I found that these modalities align perfectly with my understanding of the interplay between body, mind, and spirit. I decided to seek out a Reiki practitioner, hoping to experience the healing power of energy work.

During my first session, I lay on a massage table, surrounded by calming scents and soft music. The practitioner moved her hands gently above my body, channeling energy into me. As I closed my eyes, I felt a sense of warmth spreading through me. I entered a deep state of relaxation, and in that blissful moment, I offered a prayer of gratitude for the healing energy flowing through me. I visualized my body absorbing this energy, nourishing every cell and promoting balance.

After the session, I felt lighter, as if a burden had been lifted. I couldn't help but connect this experience to my prayer practice. I realized that both prayer and energy healing are about opening ourselves to receive the healing we seek. They invite us to trust in the process and allow the universe to guide us on our journeys.

As time went on, I integrated these practices into my life, creating a holistic approach to healing. I began to understand that my physical body, mind, and spirit are interconnected, each influencing the other. When I felt physical discomfort, I turned to prayer and meditation. When I encountered emotional challenges, I sought out energy healing and community support. This interplay of practices empowered me to take charge of my healing journey.

One evening, I reflected on my progress, feeling a deep sense of gratitude for the lessons I had learned. I recognized that healing is an ongoing process, one that requires patience, trust, and love. I understood that prayer is not just about asking for what we want; it's about cultivating a relationship with the divine, a dialogue that invites healing into our lives.

In closing, I invite you to explore the role of prayer in your own healing journey. Embrace it as a tool for connection, reflection, and transformation. Allow prayer to guide you in times of need, nurturing both your physical body and your spirit. Remember that healing is not a destination; it's a journey filled with twists and turns. By integrating prayer into your daily practice, you can cultivate a deeper understanding of the interplay between body, mind, and spirit, unlocking the healing potential that resides within you. Together, let us celebrate the power of prayer and the profound journey of holistic healing through faith.

Connecting Mind and Spirit through Faith

The first time I felt a true alignment of my mind and spirit was during a quiet morning when I found myself just sitting in silence, without any plans or expectations. It was almost accidental, a pause that I hadn't planned but one that felt profoundly right. My mind, usually busy with an endless stream of thoughts, suddenly felt calm, as if my spirit had reached over and gently pressed pause. In that moment, I felt a deep sense of wholeness, a connection that was as grounding as it was uplifting. That unplanned stillness brought a realization: this was what I had been seeking, often without realizing it—a union of mind and spirit that anchored me in faith and carried me forward with a newfound sense of purpose.

That day was only the beginning of my journey toward understanding how deeply faith could influence my mind and spirit and how the two, when harmonized, brought a profound sense of peace into my life. Until then, I had mostly approached faith intellectually, following routines and practices without always pausing to connect them to something deeper within me. But that quiet morning sparked an inner curiosity. I started exploring the role faith could play in linking my thoughts, emotions, and spiritual self in a way that felt natural and truly fulfilling.

As I began to explore this connection, I learned that it wasn't about simply following rituals or memorizing phrases; it was about feeling my way through faith, letting it seep into my mind and spirit in an authentic way. One of the most transformative aspects of this journey was learning how to silence my mind, even for a few moments each day. I found that when I quieted my thoughts, something beautiful happened. In that silence, I could feel a gentle presence—a whisper of peace that felt deeply familiar yet often overlooked. It was as if my spirit had been waiting patiently, ready to reveal truths I'd been too busy to notice.

This awareness began to change the way I experienced everyday life. My inner world felt richer, as though I had tapped into a well of insight and calm that had always been there, waiting for me to discover it. This wasn't an instant transformation; it was more like a gradual unfolding, an opening of the heart that revealed layer after layer of inner wisdom and strength. And as I leaned into this newfound connection, I started noticing the changes in my thoughts and actions. I felt more grounded, less reactive, and more able to approach life's challenges with a sense of calm and trust.

One experience stands out to me as a pivotal moment in this journey. It happened one evening when I was feeling particularly overwhelmed by a series of unexpected setbacks. My mind was racing with worries, trying to predict and control outcomes that seemed far beyond my reach. In a moment of frustration, I closed my eyes and took a deep breath, hoping to quiet my racing thoughts. In that stillness, I felt an inner nudge to pray, not just as a plea for help but as a way to align my mind with my faith.

As I began to pray, I noticed my focus shifting from the problems in front of me to a sense of presence within me. My mind slowly quieted, and I felt my spirit responding to the peace that faith brings. I let go of the need to control, allowing myself to simply rest in that moment of trust. By the end of that prayer, I felt lighter, as though a weight had been lifted from my mind. That moment taught me that faith isn't just something I turn to when I need answers; it's a source of strength that harmonizes my mind and spirit, allowing me to face challenges with a clear, grounded perspective.

This harmony between mind and spirit didn't just make me feel better during tough times; it also transformed the way I experienced joy and gratitude. When I allowed my faith to guide my thoughts, I found that simple moments took on a greater depth. I remember one morning, sitting outside with a cup of tea, watching the sun rise. Normally, my mind would be filled with the tasks of the day, but on this particular morning, I let my faith lead my thoughts. I focused on the beauty of the moment, the warmth of the sun, and the miracle of a new day. In that simple experience, I felt an overwhelming sense of gratitude, a joy that filled me in a way words can't quite capture. It was as if my mind and spirit were in perfect sync, each amplifying the other, making me feel truly alive.

Over time, I've come to see this interplay between mind and spirit as a dance, one that requires attention and intention. There are days when my mind feels scattered, busy with the demands of life, and I notice my spirit feeling a little distant. It's in those moments that I remind myself to come back to the present, to reconnect through prayer or meditation, and to allow my faith to bring me back into alignment. It's not always easy, but the effort is worth it. I've learned that just as my mind can influence my emotions, my spirit can lift my thoughts, offering a perspective that feels more grounded and expansive. Each time I reconnect in this way, I'm reminded of how faith has the power to center me, to bring a sense of calm even amidst chaos.

One of the most beautiful aspects of this journey has been discovering how my inner peace affects those around me. I noticed that when I'm grounded in my faith, others respond to that energy. Friends and family have told me that they feel a sense of calm in my presence, and that realization humbles me. It reminds me that when we nurture our connection to our spirit, we don't just benefit ourselves; we bring peace and warmth into the lives of others, often without even trying. This ripple effect has deepened my gratitude for the journey, knowing that each step I take toward inner harmony helps create a more peaceful world, one small interaction at a time.

Faith has become a guide for my thoughts, helping me to recognize and release those patterns of worry and doubt that used to control me. I've learned to pause and listen to my spirit when my mind starts to spiral, trusting that faith will guide me back to clarity. This practice has taught me that faith isn't a passive belief; it's an active choice to align my mind with my spirit, to listen to that quiet wisdom within that always knows what I need. There's a strength that comes from this alignment, a sense of wholeness that allows me to move through life with greater confidence and compassion.

There was a time when I doubted the importance of this connection, thinking that faith was something separate from my everyday thoughts and decisions. But as I've journeyed deeper, I've come to see that faith is the bridge between my mind and spirit, the thread that weaves them together into a beautiful tapestry of inner peace. This connection doesn't mean that life is always easy or that I don't face challenges. But it does mean that I approach those challenges with a sense of trust and resilience, knowing that I'm not navigating them alone.

Each day, as I continue to nurture this connection, I feel a deeper sense of purpose. I know that my faith isn't just a belief; it's a living, breathing force that shapes my thoughts, my actions, and my interactions with the world around me. It reminds me to see beyond the surface, to recognize the divine in the everyday, and to approach life with a spirit of gratitude and humility. This journey has shown me that when mind and spirit come together through faith, life becomes not just something to be endured but something to be embraced, savored, and celebrated.

In those quiet moments, when I feel the peace that only faith can bring, I'm reminded of how connected we all are, and how each of us has the power to find that inner harmony. I know now that this journey isn't about reaching some final destination; it's about continually seeking alignment, allowing faith to guide us as we navigate the twists and turns of life. With each step, I feel a deeper connection to myself, to others, and to the world around me, and I'm grateful for the gift of this journey, a journey that has transformed not only my mind and spirit but my entire way of being.

Practices for Maintaining Holistic Wellness

The day I discovered the true power of holistic wellness practices was the day I thought I'd lost everything. I'd been burning the candle at both ends for years, climbing the corporate ladder with single-minded determination. My body was running on caffeine and adrenaline, my mind was a constant whirlwind of deadlines and strategies, and my spirit... well, I'd long since forgotten I even had one. Then, in the span of 24 hours, I lost my job, my partner left me, and I found myself sitting alone in my expensive apartment, wondering how it had all gone so wrong.

That moment of crisis became the catalyst for a profound transformation in my life. As I sat there, feeling utterly lost and broken, I realized that I'd been neglecting the most important aspects of my being – my physical health, my mental well-being, and my spiritual connection. It was time for a change, and that change would come through embracing holistic wellness practices.

My journey began with a simple decision to take better care of my body. I'd always viewed exercise as a necessary evil, something to be endured for the sake of maintaining a socially acceptable appearance. But now, I approached it with a different mindset. I started with gentle yoga, allowing myself to really feel and connect with my body for perhaps the first time in years.

I'll never forget my first sun salutation sequence. As I moved through the poses, syncing my breath with each movement, I felt a strange sensation – as if I was waking up parts of myself that had long been dormant. The simple act of stretching, breathing, and moving mindfully brought me into the present moment in a way I hadn't experienced before. It wasn't just about the physical benefits; I felt a sense of peace and clarity that had eluded me for so long.

Encouraged by this experience, I delved deeper into physical practices that promoted holistic wellness. I discovered the joy of hiking in nature, feeling the earth beneath my feet and the sun on my skin. Each step became a form of moving meditation, grounding me in the present moment and connecting me to the natural world around me.

One particularly memorable hike led me to a secluded waterfall. As I stood there, feeling the mist on my face and listening to the thunderous roar of the water, I had an epiphany. I realized that my body wasn't just a vehicle to carry my brain from meeting to meeting – it was an integral part of my whole being, deserving of care, respect, and love. This realization marked a significant shift in my approach to physical wellness.

As I continued to explore physical practices, I also turned my attention to nourishing my body from within. I'd always treated food as fuel, often grabbing whatever was quickest and most convenient. Now, I began to view my diet as a form of self-care and even spiritual practice. I started cooking my own meals, paying attention to the colors, textures, and flavors of whole, natural foods.

I remember the first time I made a meal entirely from scratch, using fresh, organic ingredients. As I chopped vegetables, stirred simmering pots, and inhaled the aromatic spices, I felt a sense of connection to the food I was preparing. When I sat down to eat, I took time to appreciate each bite, savoring the flavors and feeling grateful for the nourishment. It wasn't just about the physical act of eating – it was a mindful, almost meditative experience that fed my body, mind, and spirit.

This newfound appreciation for mindful eating led me to explore fasting as a spiritual and wellness practice. I started with intermittent fasting, giving my digestive system regular breaks. To my surprise, I found that these periods of fasting brought a clarity of mind and a heightened spiritual awareness that I'd never experienced before.

One particularly profound fasting experience occurred during a three-day water fast. By the second day, as my body entered a state of ketosis, I felt an incredible sense of mental clarity and spiritual openness. Sitting in meditation during this fast, I had a vivid sensation of energy moving through my body, as if long-standing blockages were being cleared away. It was a powerful reminder of the deep connection between my physical state and my spiritual well-being.

As I continued to care for my body through mindful movement, nutrition, and fasting, I also turned my attention to nurturing my mind. Years of high-stress corporate life had left my thoughts in a constant state of chaos and negativity. I knew I needed to cultivate a more positive and balanced mental state if I wanted to achieve true holistic wellness.

Meditation became my primary tool for mental wellness. I started small, with just five minutes of focused breathing each morning. At first, it was incredibly challenging. My mind would race from thought to thought, and I'd end up feeling frustrated and discouraged. But I persevered, gradually increasing the duration of my practice.

A breakthrough came during a particularly difficult meditation session. I'd been sitting for about 15 minutes, feeling increasingly agitated by my inability to quiet my mind. Suddenly, I had a moment of insight – I realized that the goal wasn't to eliminate thoughts, but to observe them without judgment. From that moment on, my practice transformed. Instead of fighting against my thoughts, I learned to watch them come and go, like clouds passing across the sky of my consciousness.

This shift in my meditation practice had profound effects on my daily life. I found myself better able to handle stress and uncertainty. When challenges arose, instead of immediately reacting, I could pause, take a breath, and respond from a place of calm clarity. It was as if meditation had created a buffer between stimulus and response, giving me the space to choose how I wanted to engage with the world.

Journaling became another crucial practice for maintaining mental wellness. Each evening, I'd take time to reflect on my day, expressing gratitude for positive experiences and exploring any challenges or difficult emotions that had arisen. This practice of self-reflection helped me process my experiences and emotions in a healthy way, preventing the build-up of stress and negative feelings.

One evening, as I was journaling about a conflict I'd had with a friend, I had a powerful realization. As I wrote about the situation, I found myself naturally shifting from a place of anger and hurt to one of empathy and understanding. I was able to see the conflict from my friend's perspective and recognize how my own actions had contributed to the misunderstanding. This insight not only helped me resolve the conflict but also deepened my understanding of the power of self-reflection in promoting emotional healing and growth.

As I continued to explore practices for mental wellness, I discovered the transformative power of affirmations and visualization. Each morning, after my meditation, I'd spend a few minutes repeating positive affirmations and visualizing my ideal day. At first, it felt a bit silly and forced, but as I persisted, I began to notice subtle shifts in my mindset and behavior.

One affirmation that particularly resonated with me was, "I am worthy of love, health, and abundance." As I repeated this daily, I found myself making choices that aligned with this belief – taking better care of my health, setting boundaries in relationships, and pursuing opportunities for growth and abundance. It was as if by consistently affirming my worth, I was reprogramming my subconscious mind and aligning my actions with my highest good.

While I'd made significant progress in caring for my body and mind, I knew that true holistic wellness also required nurturing my spirit. This aspect of my journey was perhaps the most challenging, as I'd long since disconnected from any sense of spirituality or faith. But I was determined to explore this dimension of wellness, even if it meant stepping out of my comfort zone.

My spiritual journey began with simply spending time in nature. I'd always felt a sense of peace and connection when surrounded by trees, mountains, or the ocean, but now I approached these experiences with a more intentional, spiritual mindset. I'd sit quietly in a forest or by a stream, opening myself to the wisdom and energy of the natural world.

During one such nature meditation, sitting beneath an ancient oak tree, I had a profound experience of interconnectedness. As I sat there, eyes closed, focusing on my breath, I suddenly felt as if I could sense the life force of the tree – its roots reaching deep into the earth, its branches stretching towards the sky. In that moment, I felt a deep, intuitive understanding of my place in the web of life. I was not separate from nature, but an integral part of it.

This experience sparked a desire to explore other spiritual practices. I began attending interfaith gatherings, curious to learn about different spiritual traditions and philosophies. While I didn't align myself with any particular religion, I found wisdom and beauty in many different teachings.

One practice that particularly resonated with me was the use of prayer beads. I created my own set of beads, assigning each one a specific intention or affirmation. Each morning and evening, I'd spend time moving through the beads, focusing on each intention and allowing it to sink deep into my consciousness. This practice became a powerful tool for cultivating mindfulness, gratitude, and spiritual connection.

As I continued to explore spiritual practices, I discovered the power of ritual in maintaining holistic wellness. I created a simple morning ritual that incorporated elements of physical, mental, and spiritual wellness. I'd begin with gentle stretching and yoga, move into meditation and affirmations, and conclude with a gratitude practice and setting intentions for the day.

This morning ritual became a sacred time for me, setting the tone for my entire day. On days when I skipped or rushed through the ritual, I noticed a tangible difference in my overall well-being. It was as if this practice was aligning all aspects of my being – body, mind, and spirit – and preparing me to face the day with grace and intention.

One particularly powerful addition to my spiritual practice was the use of sound healing. I discovered the transformative power of singing bowls, tuning forks, and chanting. The vibrations seemed to resonate not just in my ears, but throughout my entire being, creating a sense of harmony and balance.

I'll never forget my first experience with a full moon sound bath. Lying on the ground, surrounded by the ethereal tones of crystal bowls and gongs, I felt as if every cell in my body was being bathed in healing vibrations. As the sound washed over me, I had a vivid sensation of energy moving through my body, clearing blockages and restoring balance. It was a profound reminder of the deep connection between sound, energy, and healing.

As I continued to explore and integrate these various practices for holistic wellness, I began to notice significant changes in all areas of my life. My physical health improved dramatically – I had more energy, slept better, and rarely got sick. My mind became clearer and more focused, and I found myself better able to handle stress and challenges. And spiritually, I felt a sense of connection and purpose that had been missing for so long.

But perhaps the most profound change was in my relationships – both with myself and with others. As I learned to care for myself in a holistic way, I found that I was better able to show up authentically in my interactions with others. I was more patient, more compassionate, and more present. My relationships deepened and became more meaningful as I brought this new sense of wholeness to my connections.

One particularly touching moment came during a conversation with my father. We'd always had a somewhat strained relationship, but as I shared with him about my journey towards holistic wellness, something shifted. He listened with genuine interest, and for the first time in years, we had a deep, heartfelt conversation. It was as if my own journey towards wholeness had created space for healing in our relationship as well.

As I reflect on my journey towards holistic wellness, I'm filled with gratitude for the practices that have transformed my life. From the physical practices of yoga and mindful eating to the mental disciplines of meditation and journaling, and the spiritual explorations of nature connection and sound healing – each practice has contributed to a more balanced, integrated sense of well-being.

I've come to understand that maintaining holistic wellness is not about perfection or adhering to a rigid set of rules. It's about cultivating awareness, making conscious choices, and continuously aligning our actions with our highest good. It's about recognizing the interconnectedness of body, mind, and spirit, and nurturing all aspects of our being.

Moreover, I've discovered that this journey towards holistic wellness is not a solitary one. As I've shared my experiences and practices with others, I've found a community of like-minded individuals all striving for greater balance and wholeness in their lives. We support and inspire each other, sharing wisdom and encouragement along the way.

To anyone embarking on their own journey towards holistic wellness, I offer this advice: Be patient and compassionate with yourself. Start small, with one or two practices that resonate with you, and allow your practice to grow organically. Listen to your body, trust your intuition, and be open to the wisdom that can come from unexpected sources.

Remember that holistic wellness is not about achieving a perfect state of health or enlightenment. It's about embracing the journey, with all its ups and downs, and continually choosing practices that nurture your whole being – body, mind, and spirit. It's about cultivating a deep sense of connection – to yourself, to others, to nature, and to something greater than yourself.

As I continue on this path of holistic wellness, I remain in awe of the profound interplay between body, mind, and spirit. Each day brings new insights, challenges, and opportunities for growth. And while the practices may evolve and change over time, the core intention remains the same – to live with greater awareness, balance, and wholeness.

In the end, I've found that the most powerful practice for maintaining holistic wellness is simply this: to approach each moment, each breath, each interaction with mindfulness and love. For it is in this state of present awareness and open-heartedness that we can truly experience the beautiful integration of body, mind, and spirit – the essence of holistic wellness.

Balancing Body, Mind, and Spirit in Daily Life

Finding balance between my body, mind, and spirit has been one of the most transformative journeys of my life. I remember a time when I felt completely out of sync, as if I were a puppet with tangled strings, struggling to find harmony in my daily existence. It was during a particularly hectic period—work deadlines loomed, personal relationships felt strained, and my inner voice echoed with self-doubt. In the midst of this chaos, I longed for balance but didn't quite know how to achieve it.

One evening, after an especially overwhelming day, I plopped down on my living room floor and closed my eyes. I took a deep breath, letting the air fill my lungs before slowly releasing it. I could feel the tension in my shoulders and the tightness in my chest. In that moment of stillness, I realized that I had been neglecting the essential aspects of myself. I focused solely on my work, pushing my body through exhaustion and ignoring the whispers of my spirit. It was clear that I needed to recalibrate, to find a way to nurture all facets of my being.

I began by setting an intention to prioritize my well-being. I wanted to create a daily practice that honored my body, mind, and spirit. The next day, I woke up a little earlier than usual, eager to embrace this new commitment. I decided to start my mornings with a blend of physical activity and mindfulness. I rolled out my yoga mat and guided myself through a gentle flow. Each movement felt like a conversation between my body and mind. I breathed deeply, and with each inhale, I invited strength and energy. With every exhale, I released the weight of my worries.

As I transitioned through poses, I noticed how the physical practice grounded me. It wasn't just about stretching my muscles; it was about connecting with my body on a deeper level. I began to listen to what my body needed, whether it was a gentle twist to release tension or a restorative pose to invite calm. I felt the energy flowing through me, and for the first time in a long while, I experienced a profound sense of connection. I realized that nurturing my body was a pivotal step in achieving balance.

After my yoga session, I turned to meditation. I found a comfortable seated position, closed my eyes, and focused on my breath. I allowed thoughts to drift in and out, but instead of getting caught up in them, I observed them like clouds passing across the sky. This practice of mindfulness became a sanctuary for me. As I sat in silence, I began to cultivate awareness of my thoughts and emotions. I learned to recognize patterns of negativity and self-doubt that often crept into my mind. With this newfound awareness, I could gently redirect my thoughts toward gratitude and positivity.

One day, while meditating, I felt a surge of inspiration. I envisioned my mind as a garden, filled with both vibrant flowers and stubborn weeds. I realized that I had the power to choose which thoughts to nurture. In that moment, I committed to tending my mental garden with love and intention. I started incorporating affirmations into my morning routine, speaking words of encouragement and strength over myself. "I am capable. I am worthy. I embrace my journey." These affirmations shifted my mindset, helping me cultivate a more positive outlook on life.

As I continued to nurture my body and mind, I recognized the importance of addressing my spirit. I sought ways to connect with my inner self and the world around me. Nature became my sanctuary. I began taking daily walks in the park, immersing myself in the beauty of the outdoors. I noticed the vibrant colors of the flowers, the rustling of leaves in the wind, and the songs of birds overhead. Each walk felt like a sacred ritual, a reminder of the interconnectedness of all living things. I breathed in the fresh air, feeling it nourish my spirit.

One afternoon, while walking through a sun-dappled forest, I stumbled upon a small clearing. I felt drawn to sit on a moss-covered log. As I closed my eyes and took in the sounds of nature, I felt a deep sense of peace wash over me. In that quiet moment, I offered a prayer of gratitude for the beauty surrounding me. I expressed my appreciation for the lessons nature teaches us—resilience, growth, and the cyclical nature of life. This experience deepened my spiritual connection and reminded me that my spirit thrives in communion with the world around me.

As I explored my spirituality, I also embraced creative expression. I picked up my paintbrush after years of neglecting my artistic side. I let my intuition guide me, allowing colors to flow freely on the canvas without judgment. Each stroke became a form of meditation, a way to express my emotions and connect with my spirit. I found joy in the process of creation, and I began to understand that nurturing my creativity was essential for my overall well-being.

Throughout this journey, I encountered moments of doubt and struggle. There were days when I felt overwhelmed by responsibilities or when self-criticism crept back in. During these times, I returned to my practices— yoga, meditation, nature walks, and creative expression. I reminded myself that balance is not a destination but a continuous journey. I learned to embrace imperfection and give myself grace on the harder days.

One particularly challenging week, I faced a series of unexpected setbacks. A project at work took an unexpected turn, testing my patience and resilience. I felt frustration rising within me, and I struggled to maintain my sense of balance. In the midst of this turmoil, I decided to take a step back and reassess. I turned to my practices, grounding myself in the knowledge that I had the tools to navigate this storm.

I rolled out my yoga mat and engaged in a more vigorous practice, allowing my body to release pent-up energy. As I transitioned through poses, I visualized the challenges as waves crashing against me, reminding myself that I could ride them rather than be overwhelmed by them. I emerged from that session feeling stronger and more centered.

Later that week, I took a moment to reflect on what I had learned. I realized that the interplay between my body, mind, and spirit was vital, especially during challenging times. I began journaling about my experiences, allowing my thoughts and feelings to flow freely onto the pages. Writing became a therapeutic outlet, a way to process my emotions and gain clarity. Through this practice, I discovered that vulnerability was not a weakness; it was a strength that allowed me to connect with my authentic self.

As I continued to cultivate balance, I also recognized the significance of community. I sought out like-minded individuals who shared my desire for holistic well-being. I joined a local wellness group that focused on mindfulness, yoga, and creative expression. The connections I formed within this community were invaluable. We shared our struggles and triumphs, supporting one another on our journeys. I felt a sense of belonging that enriched my own practice.

One evening, we gathered for a potluck, sharing nourishing meals and stories of our experiences. Around the table, I felt the warmth of connection. We took turns sharing our intentions for the upcoming month, and I was struck by the diversity of our aspirations. Some sought to deepen their meditation practice, while others aimed to explore new creative outlets. In that space, I felt a collective energy that fueled my own commitment to balance.

As I immersed myself in this community, I began to explore various modalities for healing and self-care. I attended workshops on herbalism, holistic nutrition, and energy healing. Each experience broadened my understanding of health and well-being. I learned about the importance of nourishing my body with whole foods, and I started experimenting with new recipes in my kitchen. Cooking became a joyful act of self-care, a way to honor my body and nourish my spirit.

One afternoon, I decided to host a cooking night with friends. We gathered in my kitchen, chopping vegetables and sharing laughter. As we prepared our meal together, I felt a sense of connection and joy. We shared not only food but also our stories and dreams. This experience reinforced my understanding that nourishing our bodies goes hand in hand with nurturing our relationships.

As my journey continued, I found myself reflecting on the balance I had cultivated in my life. I began to notice how my body responded positively to the care I offered it. I had more energy, and my mind felt clearer. I was better equipped to navigate challenges, and I approached life with a newfound sense of resilience. I understood that nurturing my body, mind, and spirit was not a one-time effort; it required consistent attention and intention.

One evening, I found myself sitting on my porch, watching the sunset paint the sky in hues of orange and pink. I took a moment to pause and reflect on my journey. I felt a deep sense of gratitude for the lessons I had learned about balance and harmony. I realized that each aspect of my being—body, mind, and spirit—was interconnected, and when I nurtured one, the others flourished as well.

In that moment of quiet reflection, I made a commitment to continue prioritizing balance in my life. I set intentions for the future, acknowledging that while challenges would arise, I had the tools to navigate them. I promised myself to remain curious, open to new experiences that would enrich my journey. I understood that balance is not a static state; it's an ever-evolving dance that requires awareness and self-compassion.

As I moved forward, I embraced the idea of balance as a way of life. I continued to wake up early for my yoga practice, savoring the stillness of the morning. I dedicated time to my creative pursuits, allowing my spirit to express itself freely. I ventured into nature, seeking solace in the beauty of the world around me. And I prioritized connection, nurturing my relationships with friends and family.

Through this journey, I learned that balance is not about perfection; it's about honoring my unique path. I understood that it's okay to stumble and to feel out of sync at times. What matters is the willingness to return to my practices, to recalibrate, and to embrace the ebb and flow of life.

In closing, I encourage you to explore the balance of body, mind, and spirit in your own life. Embrace the journey with curiosity and compassion. Allow yourself the grace to navigate challenges while nurturing each aspect of your being. Remember that balance is not a destination; it's a continuous dance—a beautiful interplay of self-discovery and growth. Together, let us celebrate the richness of life and the profound healing that comes from cultivating harmony within ourselves.

FACING ADVERSITY WITH GRACE: HOW FAITH GUIDES US THROUGH HARDSHIP

Understanding Adversity in the Spiritual Context

Adversity has a way of shaking us, stripping away what we thought was secure and laying bare the parts of ourselves we sometimes prefer not to examine. I still remember a particular time in my life when adversity came in like an unexpected storm, changing the course of my days and the lens through which I viewed the world. It wasn't the kind of hardship you can brush off or escape; it was deep, challenging, and it stayed with me, lingering long enough that I had to confront it head-on. As I walked through those days, I began to see how faith transformed my view of hardship and how, in ways I couldn't anticipate, it guided me through each struggle with a grace I hadn't known I possessed.

The first realization I came to was that faith doesn't prevent pain. I'd often clung to the comforting belief that somehow, being faithful might mean I'd be shielded from suffering. But when life brought me face-to-face with personal and professional challenges, I understood that faith doesn't keep us from hardship; it changes the way we endure it. My initial reaction was one of resistance, clinging to old routines and ways of thinking in an effort to regain control. I fought hard against my circumstances, wrestling with worry and doubt, questioning how life had veered off the path I had so carefully charted. It was only in the silence, in moments when I let go of my frantic need for control, that I felt a profound sense of peace. That was when I realized the deeper purpose of my struggle.

During this time, my faith felt like an anchor in a stormy sea. When everything around me seemed uncertain, it was faith that reminded me to breathe, to keep going, and to trust that even though I couldn't see the outcome, there was purpose in the journey. There were mornings I'd wake up feeling like the weight of my worries would consume me. But in those moments, I would sit in silence, close my eyes, and turn inward, letting prayer be the bridge that connected my fears to something greater than myself. In that stillness, I sensed a whisper, a quiet reminder that I wasn't alone, even in my darkest hours. This assurance became my light, a soft, steady glow that I could lean on when everything else felt too heavy.

One evening, after a particularly difficult day, I went for a walk, hoping that movement might ease my mind. I remember watching the sun setting, casting warm hues across the sky, and it struck me that no matter the challenges of the day, the world still turned, and beauty still found a way to shine through. In that simple, silent moment, I felt my perspective begin to shift. My struggles didn't disappear, but I began to see them as part of a larger picture, a narrative in which my soul was growing, adapting, and learning to hold space for both joy and sorrow. I started to understand that adversity wasn't something to be feared; it was a teacher, a force that, when embraced with grace, would carve new depths within me, depths I hadn't known existed.

As I leaned deeper into faith, I learned to ask different questions. Instead of asking, "Why is this happening to me?" I began to ask, "What is this experience teaching me?" This shift allowed me to open myself to the wisdom that only hardship could bring. I started noticing how, in moments of vulnerability, I found new strength. I began to see how setbacks forced me to reconsider my priorities, to question what I truly valued and to let go of attachments that had been weighing me down. Each struggle brought me closer to my inner self, revealing layers of resilience I hadn't tapped into before.

There were times when I felt completely worn out, moments when the adversity seemed to stretch on forever without any sign of relief. In those instances, my faith reminded me that I didn't need to carry the burden alone. I began to lean into the support of friends and family, realizing that faith is not only a solitary journey but one that we walk alongside others. I opened up to people I trusted, sharing my struggles and listening to theirs. In the simple act of connection, I found a kind of healing. It was humbling to see how each of us, in our own way, was navigating life's storms. We shared our doubts, our fears, and our faith, and in those conversations, I felt the strength that comes from knowing we're all part of a greater whole, each of us supported by a foundation of love and understanding.

One of the most profound changes that adversity brought to my life was a shift in gratitude. It may sound surprising, but hardship taught me to appreciate even the smallest blessings. In the absence of ease, I began to cherish moments of peace more deeply. Small acts of kindness, a gentle smile from a stranger, or the warmth of the sun on my face—all of these became reminders that beauty and grace still exist, even in difficult times. Each small joy felt like a gift, a reminder from life that, despite the struggles, there was still much to be grateful for. Adversity had a way of stripping away the unnecessary, leaving only what mattered most, and I found a new depth of appreciation for these simple yet profound blessings.

Looking back, I can see how my view of adversity has changed. I no longer see it as something to be avoided or feared. Instead, I see it as an integral part of my spiritual growth, a process that shapes and refines me. Adversity has taught me patience, resilience, and empathy, qualities that I may never have fully embraced without the trials that life presented. Faith, in these moments, has been more than just a belief; it has been a lifeline, a reminder that each struggle has purpose, even if I can't immediately see it.

There was a particular moment during this journey that stands out vividly in my memory. It was a night when I felt utterly lost, questioning everything I thought I knew. I remember sitting alone, overwhelmed by a feeling of isolation, and in that moment of despair, I decided to surrender fully. I stopped fighting, stopped resisting, and simply let go, allowing faith to fill the spaces where fear had been. I whispered a prayer, not for solutions but for peace, for the strength to continue even without clear answers. As I sat there, a calmness settled over me, a quiet assurance that, regardless of the outcome, I would be okay. That night, I experienced firsthand the power of faith to carry us through even the darkest moments, a feeling of grace that transcended the immediate situation and left me with a profound sense of peace.

Over time, I've come to understand that faith is not about having all the answers; it's about trusting that there's a deeper wisdom at work, guiding us through each experience. Adversity, with all its challenges, is part of that guidance. It invites us to examine our beliefs, to strengthen our convictions, and to grow in ways we may never have imagined. Faith gives us the courage to face hardship not as something to be feared, but as an opportunity to become more compassionate, more resilient, and more aligned with our true selves.

Today, I carry this understanding with me, knowing that each difficulty I encounter is part of a larger journey, one that continues to unfold with each step I take. Faith has become the lens through which I view adversity, not as an enemy but as a companion that walks beside me, helping me to see life's challenges as stepping stones rather than stumbling blocks. With this perspective, I face each new day with a renewed sense of strength, knowing that, no matter what comes my way, faith will continue to guide me, offering grace in times of hardship and teaching me the power of resilience.

In the end, adversity has shaped me in ways I never expected. It has humbled me, taught me patience, and opened my heart to a depth of compassion that I might never have known. And while I would not wish hardship upon anyone, I now see it as a gift, a teacher that has enriched my life beyond measure. I continue to walk this path, aware that more challenges will come, but I do so with a grateful heart, knowing that faith will guide me through each one, offering strength, wisdom, and peace in every season of life.

Relying on Faith during Difficult Times

I never truly understood the power of faith until I found myself standing at the edge of a precipice, staring into the abyss of despair. Life had thrown me a curveball I never saw coming, and in that moment, I realized that faith wasn't just a concept I'd learned about in Sunday school – it was the lifeline I desperately needed to cling to.

It all began on what should have been an ordinary Tuesday morning. I woke up, made my coffee, and sat down to check my emails as usual. That's when I saw it – a message from my doctor with the results of some routine tests I'd taken the week before. My heart raced as I clicked open the email, and suddenly, the world as I knew it shattered. The diagnosis was clear: I had a rare and aggressive form of cancer.

In that moment, time seemed to stand still. The mug of coffee in my hand grew cold, forgotten as I struggled to process the information before me. Questions flooded my mind: How could this happen? Why me? What would I do now? As the reality of my situation sank in, I felt a wave of fear and hopelessness wash over me.

It was in this dark moment that I first reached out to my faith. Not in any grand or dramatic way, but with a simple, desperate plea: "God, help me." As those words left my lips, I felt something shift inside me. It wasn't a miraculous cure or a sudden revelation, but a tiny spark of hope igniting in the darkness of my fear.

That spark of hope became the foundation upon which I built my journey through this unexpected and terrifying chapter of my life. As I navigated the complex world of medical treatments, second opinions, and difficult decisions, I found myself leaning more and more on my faith for strength and guidance.

One particularly challenging day stands out in my memory. I'd just finished another grueling round of chemotherapy, and the side effects were hitting me hard. Physically and emotionally drained, I curled up in my hospital bed, feeling utterly alone and defeated. It was then that I remembered a prayer my grandmother had taught me when I was a child. With nothing left to lose, I began to recite it softly:

"God, grant me the serenity to accept the things I cannot change,

Courage to change the things I can,

And wisdom to know the difference."

As I repeated these words, something remarkable happened. My racing thoughts began to slow, and a sense of calm washed over me. I realized that while I couldn't control my diagnosis or the difficult journey ahead, I could control my response to it. I could choose to face each day with grace, courage, and faith.

This realization became a turning point in my journey. Instead of viewing my illness as a punishment or a curse, I began to see it as an opportunity for growth and deepening my faith. I started to look for small blessings in each day – the kindness of a nurse, a message from a friend, or a moment of pain-free peace.

As my treatment progressed, I found myself drawn to the stories of others who had faced adversity with faith. I devoured books, listened to podcasts, and sought out support groups where people shared their experiences of relying on faith during difficult times. These stories became a source of inspiration and comfort, reminding me that I wasn't alone in my struggles.

One story that particularly resonated with me was shared by a fellow patient during a support group meeting. She spoke about how she had started a gratitude journal during her treatment, writing down three things she was thankful for each day, no matter how small. Inspired by her example, I decided to start my own gratitude practice.

At first, it was challenging to find things to be grateful for when I was feeling so sick and scared. But as I persevered, I began to notice more and more blessings in my life. Some days, my list included things like "the sun shining through my window" or "the taste of fresh water." Other days, I found myself grateful for deeper things – the unwavering support of my family, the skill and compassion of my medical team, or a moment of clarity and peace during prayer.

This daily practice of gratitude became a powerful tool in maintaining my faith and positive outlook. It helped me shift my focus from what I had lost or was struggling with to the abundance of blessings still present in my life. Even on my darkest days, when fear and pain threatened to overwhelm me, I could always find at least one thing to be thankful for.

As my treatment continued, I found myself drawn to explore different aspects of my faith that I had never delved into before. I began to study sacred texts more deeply, not just reading the words but really pondering their meaning and how they applied to my life. I started practicing meditation, using it as a way to quiet my anxious mind and connect more deeply with my spiritual side.

One meditation practice that became particularly meaningful to me involved visualizing myself surrounded by healing light. As I sat quietly, eyes closed, I would imagine a warm, golden light enveloping my body, filling every cell with healing energy. I would picture this light pushing out the darkness of disease and fear, replacing it with strength, hope, and faith.

At first, this visualization felt a bit forced and awkward. But as I continued to practice, it became easier and more natural. There were times during my treatment when I would use this visualization to help me through particularly difficult procedures or moments of intense anxiety. It became a powerful tool for maintaining my faith and positive outlook, even in the face of physical discomfort and fear.

As I continued on my journey, I began to notice subtle changes in my relationships with others. My faith wasn't just sustaining me through my personal struggles; it was also influencing how I interacted with the world around me. I found myself becoming more patient, more compassionate, and more willing to see the good in others.

One day, as I sat in the waiting room before a scan, I noticed a young woman who looked terrified. Without thinking, I smiled at her and struck up a conversation. As we talked, I shared a bit about my own journey and how my faith had helped me through the tough times. To my surprise, she opened up about her own fears and doubts. By the time we were called for our appointments, we had formed a connection, and I could see that she seemed a little more at peace.

This interaction made me realize that my faith wasn't just about getting through my own struggles – it was also about being a light for others. From that day on, I made a conscious effort to reach out to others in the waiting rooms, treatment areas, and support groups. Sometimes it was just a smile or a kind word, other times it was sharing my story or listening to theirs. Each of these interactions strengthened my own faith and reminded me that even in the midst of my own trials, I could still be a source of hope and comfort for others.

As my treatment progressed, there were certainly moments of doubt and fear. There were days when the physical pain and emotional exhaustion made it hard to hold onto my faith. But in those moments, I would often think back to that first day when I received my diagnosis, and how that simple plea for help had ignited a spark of hope within me.

I began to see my faith not as a magic solution that would instantly fix everything, but as a steady companion on this difficult journey. It was the voice that whispered "keep going" when I felt like giving up, the comfort that held me when I cried in the middle of the night, and the hope that helped me envision a future beyond my current struggles.

One particularly powerful moment came towards the end of my treatment. I had just received news that my latest scans showed significant improvement, and for the first time in months, I felt a real sense of hope for my future. As I sat in the hospital chapel, overwhelmed with gratitude, I found myself reflecting on the journey I had been through.

I realized that my faith hadn't just helped me survive this ordeal – it had transformed me. The person sitting in that chapel was not the same one who had received that life-altering email months ago. My faith had given me strength I didn't know I possessed, taught me to find joy in the smallest moments, and shown me the incredible power of hope and love.

As I continued to recover and regain my strength, I felt a strong calling to share my experiences with others. I started volunteering at the hospital, offering support and encouragement to patients who were just beginning their own journeys. I found that sharing my story of faith and resilience often gave others hope in their darkest moments.

One day, I met a young man who had just received a similar diagnosis to mine. The fear and despair in his eyes mirrored what I had felt all those months ago. As I shared my story with him, I could see a glimmer of hope begin to spark in his eyes. Before I left, he asked me, "How did you do it? How did you keep your faith when things got really tough?"

I thought carefully before answering, wanting to be honest about both the challenges and the blessings of relying on faith during difficult times. Finally, I said, "It wasn't always easy. There were days when my faith felt as fragile as a candle flame in a storm. But I learned that faith isn't about never doubting or never being afraid. It's about choosing to believe even when it's hard, about finding hope in the darkest moments, and about trusting that there's a greater purpose to our struggles, even when we can't see it."

As I continue on my journey of recovery and growth, I'm constantly amazed by the ways in which my faith continues to guide and sustain me. It's not just about believing in a higher power or adhering to certain religious practices. It's about cultivating a deep sense of trust in the universe, finding meaning in our struggles, and maintaining hope even in the face of seemingly insurmountable odds.

I've learned that faith is not a static thing, but a living, growing part of who we are. It's shaped by our experiences, strengthened by our challenges, and expressed through our actions. My faith today is both stronger and more flexible than it was before my illness. It's less about rigid beliefs and more about an open-hearted trust in the goodness of life, even when that goodness is hard to see.

One of the most profound lessons I've learned is the importance of community in sustaining faith during difficult times. While my personal relationship with my faith was crucial, the support and encouragement of others played an equally important role. The friends who prayed with me, the support group members who shared their own stories of faith and resilience, and the strangers who offered kind words or gestures – all of these became part of my faith journey.

I've come to see faith not as a solitary pursuit, but as something that flourishes in connection with others. It's in sharing our struggles and our hopes, in supporting each other through difficult times, that our faith grows stronger and more resilient.

As I reflect on my journey, I'm filled with a deep sense of gratitude – not just for my recovery, but for the growth and transformation that came through this challenging experience. My faith guided me through the darkest times, helping me to find meaning and purpose in my struggles. It taught me to appreciate the beauty of each moment, to find strength I didn't know I had, and to see the interconnectedness of all life.

To anyone facing their own trials and wondering how to maintain faith in difficult times, I would say this: Be gentle with yourself. Faith isn't about being perfect or never doubting. It's about taking one step at a time, trusting that there's a path forward even when you can't see it clearly. Look for the small blessings in each day, lean on others when you need to, and remember that your struggles don't define you – it's how you respond to them that matters.

Above all, remember that faith is not just about getting through the hard times – it's about how we grow and transform through our challenges. It's about becoming more compassionate, more resilient, and more connected to the world around us. It's about learning to see the divine in every moment, even the difficult ones.

As I continue on my journey, I carry with me the lessons learned during those challenging months. My faith remains a guiding light, helping me navigate not just the big crises but the everyday challenges of life. It reminds me to approach each day with gratitude, to treat others with kindness and compassion, and to trust in the unfolding of life's journey.

I've learned that facing adversity with grace doesn't mean we never struggle or feel afraid. It means we choose to keep moving forward, to keep believing in the possibility of better days ahead, even when the path is difficult. It means we allow our challenges to open our hearts rather than close them, to deepen our connection to others and to the world around us.

In the end, I've found that faith is not just about believing in something greater than ourselves. It's about recognizing the greatness within us – the strength, resilience, and capacity for love that we all possess. It's about trusting in the journey of life, with all its ups and downs, and knowing that each experience, even the painful ones, offers an opportunity for growth and transformation.

As I look to the future, I do so with a heart full of hope and gratitude. My faith, tested and strengthened by adversity, continues to guide me forward. It reminds me daily that life, with all its challenges and blessings, is a precious gift to be cherished and lived fully. And for that, I am eternally grateful.

Prayers for Patience and Endurance

Patience and endurance have often felt like elusive qualities, especially during the most challenging times of my life. I remember a moment when I faced a particularly trying period—one that tested my resolve in ways I never imagined. It was a season of uncertainty, filled with unexpected twists that left me feeling anxious and overwhelmed. I found myself praying for patience and endurance, seeking a way to navigate the storm with grace.

One evening, as I sat in my dimly lit living room, I felt the weight of the world pressing down on me. Bills piled up on the kitchen counter, my job felt increasingly demanding, and personal relationships required more effort than I had energy for. I sank into my couch, closed my eyes, and took a deep breath. In that moment, I realized how much I needed to surrender to something greater than myself. I turned my thoughts toward prayer, quietly asking for the strength to endure and the patience to navigate the challenges ahead.

As I prayed, I visualized my struggles as waves crashing against a sturdy cliff. I pictured myself standing firm, rooted in the earth, even as the waves threatened to pull me under. I could almost hear the gentle whispers of reassurance, reminding me that I was not alone. This simple act of prayer became a lifeline, grounding me in the knowledge that there was a purpose to my struggles.

In the days that followed, I made a conscious effort to incorporate prayer into my daily routine. Each morning, I would wake up, take a moment to center myself, and express my intentions for the day. I found solace in affirmations like "I embrace challenges with grace" and "I trust the process of growth." These phrases became a mantra, a way to remind myself that patience and endurance were not just qualities I wished for; they were traits I could cultivate with intention.

There were moments when my resolve wavered. One particularly tough week, I faced a barrage of challenges. A project at work went awry, leading to late nights and mounting stress. I felt my patience wearing thin, and in those moments, I turned to prayer. I sought refuge in the quiet of my mind, asking for clarity and strength. I learned to listen during these prayers, allowing my heart to guide me toward the answers I needed.

One evening, after a long day at work, I decided to take a walk in my neighborhood. The sun began to set, casting a golden hue over everything.

As I strolled, I reflected on my day and the challenges I faced. With each step, I voiced my frustrations and fears in prayer. I felt the tension in my body begin to ease, and I realized that expressing my thoughts aloud helped me process my emotions.

The beauty of nature surrounded me—the vibrant colors of the flowers, the gentle rustle of leaves in the wind, and the distant sound of laughter from children playing. In that moment, I felt a sense of connection to something larger than myself. My worries began to fade as I reminded myself that life ebbs and flows, just like the seasons. I understood that patience is a part of the process, a necessary ingredient in the journey of growth.

During this time, I also began to recognize the importance of community in cultivating patience and endurance. I reached out to friends and family, sharing my struggles and seeking support. I found that vulnerability created a space for connection, allowing others to share their own experiences of facing adversity. I listened as they recounted their stories, and in those moments, I realized us all face challenges that test our resolve.

One evening, a close friend invited me over for dinner. As we sat around the table, I shared my recent struggles and the prayers I had been offering for patience and endurance. She nodded, her eyes reflecting understanding. "You know," she said, "I've been in that place too. Sometimes, it helps to remember that it's okay to take things one step at a time." Her words resonated deeply within me. I recognized that endurance doesn't mean pushing through without pause; it means allowing ourselves the grace to navigate our journey in our own time.

Inspired by our conversation, I decided to create a gratitude jar. Each evening, I would write down moments of patience I had experienced during the day, whether they were small victories or significant breakthroughs. I found joy in reflecting on the positive moments, no matter how fleeting. This practice shifted my perspective, helping me see that patience and endurance manifest in everyday life.

One day, as I prepared to write in my gratitude jar, I stumbled upon an old photo album. I flipped through the pages, reminiscing about moments that shaped me. I came across pictures from a hiking trip I took years ago. I remembered the physical challenges I faced, the steep inclines that tested my endurance. Yet, with each step, I felt a sense of accomplishment. I recalled how the breathtaking views at the summit made every struggle worthwhile. This memory ignited a spark within me, reminding me that endurance often leads to beautiful outcomes.

As weeks turned into months, I discovered that my prayers for patience and endurance were evolving into something deeper. I began to embrace the idea that these qualities were not just about enduring hardship; they were about appreciating the journey. I learned to celebrate the small victories, whether it was completing a challenging project at work or simply taking a moment to breathe amidst the chaos.

One afternoon, I found myself sitting in my backyard, surrounded by the sounds of nature. I poured my heart into prayer, expressing gratitude for the lessons learned during difficult times. I acknowledged the moments when I felt frustrated, but I also celebrated the strength I discovered within myself. I recognized that endurance is a muscle we build over time, one that grows stronger with each challenge we face.

During this period of reflection, I also began to explore the concept of mindfulness. I discovered how being present in each moment could help me cultivate both patience and endurance. I started practicing mindfulness during my daily activities, whether it was savoring a cup of tea or taking a few minutes to breathe deeply before diving into work. I found that these small moments of awareness helped me feel more grounded and centered, fostering a sense of calm even amidst the busyness of life.

One evening, after a particularly stressful day, I decided to treat myself to a quiet night in. I lit candles, brewed herbal tea, and settled onto the couch with a good book. As I read, I felt a sense of peace enveloping me. In that moment, I realized that self-care plays a crucial role in nurturing patience and endurance. I learned that taking time for myself doesn't mean neglecting responsibilities; it means fueling my spirit so that I can face challenges with renewed energy.

As I continued my journey, I encountered new challenges that tested my patience in unexpected ways. A family member faced health issues, and I felt a surge of fear and anxiety. I found myself praying fervently, asking for strength for both myself and my loved one. I turned to my community for support, sharing my concerns with friends who offered their love and encouragement. In those moments, I realized that endurance often means leaning on others when the weight of the world feels too heavy to bear alone.

I learned that it's okay to ask for help, to share our burdens with those we trust. One evening, I gathered a small group of friends for a prayer circle. We sat in a circle, holding hands and sharing our intentions for healing and strength. As we prayed together, I felt a powerful sense of connection. It was as if we were weaving a tapestry of support, each thread representing love, compassion, and understanding. In that sacred space, I understood that we are all interconnected in our struggles and triumphs.

Over time, I began to see the fruits of my prayers for patience and endurance manifest in my life. I found myself approaching challenges with a newfound sense of calm. When obstacles arose, I no longer felt overwhelmed; instead, I embraced them as opportunities for growth. I learned to breathe through the moments of uncertainty and trust that everything would unfold in its own time.

One morning, while journaling, I reflected on my journey. I wrote about the ways in which prayer had become a cornerstone of my life. I acknowledged the moments of struggle but celebrated the resilience I had developed. I recognized that my prayers were not just requests for strength; they had evolved into a deeper relationship with faith—a relationship built on trust, surrender, and gratitude.

As I continued to cultivate patience and endurance, I realized that this journey was ongoing. Life would inevitably present new challenges, but I felt more equipped to face them. I understood that my prayers were a source of strength, a reminder that I could navigate adversity with grace.

In closing, I invite you to explore the power of prayer for patience and endurance in your own life. Embrace the journey with an open heart, knowing that challenges are opportunities for growth. Allow your prayers to be a source of strength, guiding you through the storms of life. Remember that you are not alone; we are all interconnected in our experiences. Together, let us face adversity with grace, trusting in the process of growth and the wisdom that emerges from our struggles.

Finding Lessons in Hardship

There's something unexpected about the way hardship sneaks into life, catching us off guard, pushing us in directions we never planned. I can still remember a time when adversity seemed relentless, challenging me in ways I hadn't known were possible. In those difficult days, I found myself questioning, struggling to see beyond the immediate struggle, wondering why life had taken this path. But as I leaned more into my faith, something transformative happened—I began to see the experiences as part of a larger purpose. What initially seemed like overwhelming obstacles slowly began revealing hidden lessons, shaping me, and showing me that hardship, while painful, can be one of life's greatest teachers.

When hardship first enters your life, it's tempting to respond with resistance. I know I did. I wanted to force things back to the way they were, to ignore the struggle and try to control the outcome. But the more I fought, the more exhausted I became. There came a moment when I felt myself breaking under the weight of it all, feeling as though I had no more strength left to resist. That was when I decided to surrender—not to the hardship itself, but to faith, to the idea that there was something greater than my own limited understanding at work. In letting go, I felt a calmness wash over me, a reminder that, even in my weakest moments, I wasn't alone. My faith gave me the courage to sit with the pain, to be present with the difficulty, and to start looking for the lessons hidden within.

As the days went on, I realized that hardship was teaching me patience in a way nothing else could. Patience isn't something that comes naturally to me, and I had always been someone who wanted answers, clarity, and a clear path forward. But adversity doesn't provide those things on demand. It asks us to wait, to trust the process even when it feels like nothing is happening. In one particularly challenging situation, I was waiting for resolution, and every day felt like an exercise in patience. I wanted answers, solutions, and a way to move forward. But the waiting stretched on, longer than I thought I could bear. During this time, my faith kept me grounded. It reminded me that growth doesn't happen on a strict timeline and that there's value in the in-between spaces where we have to trust without knowing.

In these moments of waiting, I found that faith became a source of comfort and strength, a place to lean when everything else felt uncertain. I would sit quietly, breathe deeply, and let myself sink into a sense of peace, trusting that even in the stillness, something was happening beneath the surface. Over time, I learned that patience isn't about passivity; it's about surrendering our need for control and allowing life to unfold as it's meant to. That understanding has stayed with me, reminding me that even when I feel stuck, there is movement happening, growth that I might not see but can feel deep down.

One of the most unexpected lessons that hardship taught me was the importance of vulnerability. During a particularly difficult season, I found myself withdrawing from others, thinking that I had to face my struggles alone. I didn't want to burden anyone else with my problems, and I was afraid that if I opened up, I might be seen as weak. But over time, I realized that this isolation only made things harder. I needed connection, support, the reassurance that comes from sharing our burdens with those who care about us. It took courage to open up, to admit that I didn't have all the answers that I was struggling. And when I finally did, I was met with an outpouring of love and understanding that I hadn't anticipated.

Sharing my struggles with others allowed me to see that vulnerability is not a sign of weakness; it's a strength. It connects us, reminds us that we're all human, all navigating our own challenges. My faith encouraged me to trust in the strength of community, to lean on the people around me, and to accept the kindness that was offered. Through this, I learned that we're not meant to walk the path of hardship alone. We're meant to support one another, to remind each other that, no matter how heavy the burden, there is always someone willing to help carry it.

Another lesson that hardship revealed was the value of gratitude. It sounds almost counterintuitive—to find gratitude in the middle of pain and difficulty—but it was precisely in those moments of struggle that I became more aware of the blessings I might have overlooked otherwise. There were times when I felt completely overwhelmed, weighed down by the challenges I was facing. And yet, in the midst of the hardship, I began to notice small things that brought me comfort—a kind word from a friend, a moment of peace in nature, the warmth of the sun on my face. These moments, small as they were, became lifelines. They reminded me that even in the darkest times, there is light if we're willing to look for it.

One particular memory stands out to me. I was walking through a particularly challenging season, feeling completely worn out, and I happened to come across a beautiful field of wildflowers. The colors, the simplicity, the quiet beauty—it was exactly what I needed at that moment. That experience taught me that gratitude doesn't require everything to be perfect; it only requires us to open our hearts to the good that still exists, even when life feels overwhelming. In the quiet presence of those wildflowers, I felt a sense of peace and connection that helped me move forward, one small step at a time. Gratitude became my way of grounding myself, of reminding myself that, despite the hardship, there was still so much to be thankful for.

Hardship also taught me resilience, a strength that I hadn't fully understood before. When life is easy, it's tempting to assume that strength is something you either have or don't have. But adversity reveals just how capable we are of enduring, of finding ways to adapt, to keep moving even when the road is steep. There were moments when I didn't think I could go on, times when the weight of my struggles felt too heavy to bear. But each time, my faith reminded me that resilience isn't about never feeling tired or discouraged.

It's about finding the courage to get back up, to keep going, even when it feels impossible.

Faith taught me to trust in a strength beyond my own, to lean on a higher power when my own energy was depleted. In those moments, I found a resilience that surprised me, a quiet strength that carried me through the toughest days. I began to see myself differently, not as someone who was defined by the hardship but as someone who was being refined by it. Each challenge, each setback, became a stepping stone, a part of a journey that was shaping me into a stronger, more compassionate person.

One of the final lessons that hardship taught me was humility. It's easy to go through life with a sense of control, believing that we have the power to shape our destiny. But when life throws us challenges beyond our control, we're reminded of our limitations, of the unpredictability that is woven into the fabric of life. This humility, far from being a burden, became a gift. It reminded me that I'm part of something greater than myself, that there is a wisdom and order to life that I might not fully understand. Instead of trying to force my way through challenges, I learned to approach them with an open heart, with a willingness to learn, to grow, to let go of my ego and accept the guidance that life was offering.

Looking back, I see that adversity was a transformative force in my life, one that taught me lessons I might never have learned otherwise. It showed me the power of patience, the strength of vulnerability, the grounding nature of gratitude, the quiet resilience that lies within each of us, and the humility that allows us to surrender to something greater than ourselves. Faith was my constant companion on this journey, a source of comfort and strength that helped me navigate the darkest times with grace.

Today, I carry these lessons with me, knowing that life will continue to bring challenges, that hardship is not something to be feared but embraced. With each new difficulty, I remind myself that there is purpose in the pain, that there are lessons waiting to be uncovered. Faith has shown me that hardship, while painful, is also a teacher, a guide that helps us grow in ways we might not have chosen but that ultimately shape us into who we're meant to be.

Now, when I encounter challenges, I approach them with a different mindset. Instead of resisting or feeling defeated, I ask myself, "What can I learn from this? How can this experience help me grow?" This perspective has changed the way I view adversity, allowing me to face it not with fear but with a sense of openness and curiosity. I trust that each hardship is part of a larger journey, a process of growth and transformation that brings me closer to my true self.

Faith continues to guide me, offering strength in moments of weakness, comfort in times of sorrow, and a gentle reminder that, no matter how difficult the journey, there is always a purpose. Through faith, I've learned that hardship is not the end of the story but a chapter that deepens our understanding, shapes our character, and prepares us for the next stage of life's journey. In facing adversity with grace, I've discovered a profound peace, a resilience that carries me forward, and a gratitude that enriches my life in ways I never could have imagined.

Emerging Stronger Through Faith

I never imagined that a single phone call could shatter my world and rebuild it in ways I couldn't have foreseen. Yet, on that crisp autumn morning, as I answered my cell with one hand while stirring my coffee with the other, I heard the words that would change everything: "I'm sorry, but we're going to have to let you go."

In that moment, I felt as if the ground had disappeared beneath my feet. The company I'd devoted fifteen years of my life to, the career I'd built with painstaking effort, was suddenly gone. As the reality of my situation sank in, a wave of panic threatened to overwhelm me. How would I pay my bills? What would I tell my family? Where would I go from here?

It was in this moment of despair that I found myself instinctively turning to faith. Not in a grand, dramatic gesture, but in a quiet, almost desperate whisper: "Please, give me strength." As those words left my lips, I felt a subtle shift within me. It wasn't an immediate solution to my problems, but a tiny spark of hope igniting in the darkness of my fear.

That spark became the foundation upon which I would rebuild not just my career, but my entire approach to life. As I navigated the unfamiliar and often terrifying landscape of unemployment, I found myself leaning more and more on my faith for guidance and support.

One particularly challenging day stands out in my memory. I'd just returned from another fruitless job interview, my spirits at an all-time low. As I sat in my car, fighting back tears of frustration, I remembered a practice my grandmother had taught me years ago. She'd always said that in times of trouble, we should count our blessings.

At first, it felt almost impossible to find anything to be grateful for. But as I forced myself to think, I began to see small glimmers of light in the darkness. I was grateful for the roof over my head, for the support of my family, for the skills and experience I'd gained over the years. As I continued this exercise, I felt my despair slowly giving way to a cautious optimism.

This moment marked a turning point in my journey. Instead of viewing my job loss as a catastrophe, I began to see it as an opportunity for growth and transformation. I started to look for ways to use this unexpected free time to deepen my faith and explore new possibilities.

I began each day with a simple prayer, asking for guidance and the strength to face whatever challenges lay ahead. This ritual, though small, helped center me and gave me a sense of purpose as I tackled the daunting task of rebuilding my career.

As weeks turned into months, I found my faith being tested in ways I never expected. There were days when rejection letters piled up, when my savings dwindled alarmingly, when the future seemed bleak and uncertain. In these moments, I clung to my faith like a lifeline, reminding myself that this too shall pass.

One particularly difficult evening, after receiving yet another rejection, I decided to take a walk to clear my head. As I strolled through my neighborhood, lost in thought, I found myself drawn to a small community garden I'd never really noticed before. Curiosity piqued, I wandered in.

The garden was a riot of colors and scents, vegetables and flowers growing side by side in neat beds. As I admired the thriving plants, an elderly woman approached me with a warm smile. "First time here?" she asked. When I nodded, she introduced herself as Maria, the garden's caretaker.

We struck up a conversation, and before I knew it, I was pouring out my story to this kind stranger. Maria listened patiently, nodding in understanding. When I finished, she gently took my hand and led me to a small plot in the corner of the garden.

"See these tomato plants?" she said, gesturing to some scraggly-looking vines. "A month ago, they were barely surviving. But with care, patience, and faith, look at them now." She pointed to the tiny green tomatoes beginning to form on the vines.

In that moment, I felt as if a veil had been lifted from my eyes. I saw my own situation reflected in those tomato plants - struggling, yes, but with the potential for growth and fruitfulness. Maria's simple lesson in gardening became a powerful metaphor for my own journey of faith and resilience.

Inspired by this encounter, I began volunteering at the community garden. As I tended to the plants, I found myself drawing parallels between gardening and my own life. Just as each plant required different care and conditions to thrive, I realized that my own growth might take unexpected forms.

This realization led me to explore new directions I'd never considered before. I started taking online courses in fields I'd always been curious about but never had time to pursue. I reached out to old contacts, not just for job leads, but to reconnect and offer my help where I could.

As I immersed myself in these new activities, I began to notice a change in myself. The desperation that had initially driven my job search began to fade, replaced by a sense of purpose and curiosity. I wasn't just looking for a job anymore; I was seeking a path that aligned with my values and allowed me to make a meaningful contribution.

My faith, which had initially been a source of comfort in difficult times, was evolving into a guiding principle for my life. I found myself making decisions not based on fear or desperation, but on a deep-seated trust that I was being led towards something greater than I could imagine.

This newfound perspective was put to the test when I received a job offer that, on paper, seemed perfect. It was in my field, offered a good salary, and would have solved my immediate financial concerns. Yet, as I considered the offer, I felt an unexpected hesitation.

I spent a sleepless night wrestling with the decision. On one hand, the practical part of me screamed to take the job and end this period of uncertainty. On the other, a quiet voice - the voice of faith I'd come to recognize - whispered that this wasn't the right path.

In the end, I made the difficult decision to turn down the offer. It was terrifying, and I spent the next few days questioning my sanity. But deep down, I felt a sense of peace that told me I'd made the right choice.

Just a week later, I received an email that would change everything. A small non-profit organization was looking for someone to help them develop a community outreach program. The job description seemed tailor-made for my skills and experience, but more than that, it resonated with the values and sense of purpose I'd discovered during my period of unemployment.

As I interviewed for the position, I felt a sense of alignment I'd never experienced before. This wasn't just a job; it was an opportunity to make a real difference in people's lives. When I was offered the position, I accepted with a joy and gratitude that went far beyond relief at ending my unemployment.

Looking back now, I can see how my journey of faith during that difficult period prepared me for this new chapter in my life. The resilience I'd developed, the ability to find hope in challenging times, the willingness to explore new paths - all of these became invaluable assets in my new role.

My work with the non-profit brought me into contact with people facing their own struggles - job loss, homelessness, addiction. I found that my own experience of relying on faith during hardship allowed me to connect with these individuals in a deep and meaningful way.

One encounter particularly stands out in my memory. I was working with a young man named Jake who had recently lost his job and was struggling to provide for his family. As we talked about his situation, I saw in his eyes the same fear and desperation I had once felt.

Drawing on my own experience, I shared with Jake how my faith had guided me through similar challenges. I encouraged him to look for the blessings in his life, no matter how small, and to trust that this difficult period was preparing him for something greater.

Over the next few months, I watched as Jake slowly rebuilt his life. He started by volunteering at our organization, which led to new connections and eventually a job opportunity. Seeing the transformation in Jake - not just in his circumstances, but in his outlook on life - was profoundly moving. It reinforced my belief that our hardships, when faced with faith and grace, can become stepping stones to personal growth and a deeper sense of purpose.

As I continued my work, I began to see more and more how my own journey of faith was intertwined with the lives of those I was helping. Each person's story of struggle and resilience became a reminder of the power of faith to guide us through difficult times.

I started incorporating elements of spiritual support into our programs, always respecting each individual's personal beliefs. We introduced optional meditation sessions, created spaces for reflection and prayer, and encouraged participants to explore their own sources of inner strength and guidance.

The impact of these initiatives was profound. People who had come to us feeling hopeless and alone began to find a sense of community and purpose. They supported each other, shared their struggles and victories, and slowly began to rebuild their lives on a foundation of faith and mutual care.

As our programs grew and evolved, I found my own faith deepening and expanding. I was no longer just relying on faith to get me through hard times; I was actively living it out in my daily work and interactions. The boundaries between my personal spiritual life and my professional role began to blur in the most beautiful way.

One day, as I was leaving the office after a particularly challenging but rewarding day, I bumped into Maria, the gardener who had given me that crucial lesson months ago. She greeted me with a warm smile and asked how I was doing.

As I shared with her the journey I'd been on since our first encounter, her eyes lit up with understanding and joy. "You see," she said, gesturing to the thriving community garden behind her, "sometimes we need to be pruned back to grow stronger. Your faith was the root that kept you grounded, allowing you to flourish in new and unexpected ways."

Her words struck a deep chord within me. I realized that my period of unemployment, as painful as it had been, was indeed a kind of pruning. It had cut away the parts of my life that were no longer serving me, allowing new growth to emerge.

This perspective has stayed with me, shaping how I view challenges and setbacks. I've come to see adversity not as a punishment or a curse, but as an opportunity for growth and renewal. My faith, tested and strengthened through hardship, has become a wellspring of resilience and hope that I can draw upon in all aspects of my life.

As I reflect on my journey, I'm filled with a profound sense of gratitude. Gratitude for the challenges that pushed me to grow, for the people who supported and guided me along the way, and for the faith that sustained me through it all.

To anyone facing their own trials and wondering how to maintain faith in difficult times, I would say this: Trust the process. Even when you can't see the way forward, have faith that each experience is shaping you for a greater purpose. Look for the lessons and blessings in your struggles, no matter how small they may seem. And remember that faith isn't just about believing in something greater than ourselves - it's about recognizing the strength and resilience within us.

Most importantly, don't be afraid to let your faith guide you in new and unexpected directions. The path it leads you on may not be the one you originally envisioned, but it may just be the one that brings you the most growth, fulfillment, and joy.

As I continue on my own journey, I carry with me the lessons learned during those challenging months. My faith remains a guiding light, helping me navigate not just the big crises but the everyday challenges of life. It reminds me to approach each day with gratitude, to treat others with kindness and compassion, and to trust in the unfolding of life's journey.

I've learned that emerging stronger through faith doesn't mean we never struggle or feel afraid. It means we choose to keep moving forward, to keep believing in the possibility of better days ahead, even when the path is difficult. It means we allow our challenges to open our hearts rather than close them, to deepen our connection to others and to the world around us.

In the end, I've found that faith is not just about believing in something greater than ourselves. It's about recognizing the greatness within us - the strength, resilience, and capacity for love that we all possess. It's about trusting in the journey of life, with all its ups and downs, and knowing that each experience, even the painful ones, offers an opportunity for growth and transformation.

As I look to the future, I do so with a heart full of hope and gratitude. My faith, tested and strengthened by adversity, continues to guide me forward. It reminds me daily that life, with all its challenges and blessings, is a precious gift to be cherished and lived fully. And for that, I am eternally grateful.

SPIRITUAL HEALING IN RELATIONSHIPS: MENDING BONDS THROUGH PRAYER

The Importance of Healing in Relationships

I never truly understood the depth of healing in relationships until I found myself in the middle of one that was breaking. The cracks had been there for a while, but they became more visible as misunderstandings piled up and unspoken feelings started to drift to the surface. There was this gnawing sense of something slipping away, and I couldn't help but feel like I was losing a part of myself. I had always believed in the strength of love, but in that moment, I realized that love alone wasn't enough. Healing—deep, spiritual healing—was the missing piece, the one thing that could mend the wounds neither of us had fully acknowledged.

I grew up believing that relationships are about connection, understanding, and care, but rarely did I think about the importance of healing within them. We often talk about love, commitment, and forgiveness, but healing is the thread that holds everything together, especially when things fall apart. I learned this lesson firsthand when I was in a long-term relationship that, over time, had become weighed down by misunderstandings and unresolved hurts. The early days were filled with excitement and shared dreams, but as the years went by, the emotional baggage we had each brought into the relationship began to take its toll.

What I had failed to realize at the time was that each of us carried wounds —some from our pasts, others created within the relationship itself—and we hadn't fully healed from them. In my mind, I thought we could just move on, that time would naturally mend things. But I quickly discovered that time alone doesn't heal; it's the conscious effort we put into healing that makes the difference. It wasn't until the arguments became more frequent and the distance between us grew more pronounced that I realized we needed something more than just apologies or attempts to patch things up. We needed healing on a deeper level, one that would reach the spiritual and emotional core of our connection.

I remember one evening, after another exhausting argument, I felt this overwhelming sense of hopelessness. We were going in circles, saying the same things over and over without really listening or understanding each other. In that moment, I turned inward, seeking solace in prayer. I had always been someone who found comfort in my faith, but I hadn't fully understood the power of prayer when it came to relationships. That night, I didn't pray for the argument to end or for us to simply stop fighting—I prayed for healing. I prayed for clarity, for the ability to see beyond the hurt and the pain, for the strength to forgive not just my partner but also myself.

As I prayed, something shifted within me. It wasn't an instant solution to our problems, but there was this sense of peace, a quiet voice reminding me that healing takes time, patience, and openness. I began to see that our struggles weren't just about the present moment but were also rooted in deeper issues we hadn't addressed. My partner had his own wounds, just as I had mine. Instead of focusing on who was right or wrong, I started to see the pain beneath the surface, the unspoken fears and insecurities that were driving our actions.

In the days that followed, I continued to pray—not just for our relationship but for my own healing. I realized that I had been carrying emotional scars from past experiences that had nothing to do with my partner, but they were affecting how I interacted in the relationship. The more I prayed, the more I felt called to address these wounds, to acknowledge them, and to allow the healing process to begin. Prayer became a way for me to open up to the possibility of transformation, to release the need for control and to trust that healing was possible, even if it didn't happen overnight.

It wasn't easy, and there were moments when I doubted whether we could truly heal from the damage that had been done. But faith, for me, was the anchor that kept me grounded during those difficult times. I learned that healing in relationships isn't about forgetting the pain or pretending it never happened. It's about facing it head-on, with a willingness to be vulnerable, to forgive, and to rebuild from a place of honesty and love.

There was a particular moment that stands out in my mind—one that marked a turning point in our journey toward healing. We were sitting in silence after another long conversation, both emotionally drained but somehow more connected than we had been in months. I took a deep breath and said something that had been weighing on my heart for a long time. "I don't want to keep carrying this hurt. I want us to heal—together." My partner looked at me, and for the first time in what felt like forever, I saw understanding in his eyes. It wasn't just about the words I had spoken; it was about the energy behind them, the intention to heal rather than to blame or to win.

In that moment, I realized that healing in relationships requires both people to be willing to do the work. It's not enough for one person to seek healing while the other remains stuck in old patterns. We both had to be open to the process, to be willing to let go of pride and defensiveness, and to focus on mending the bond between us. It took time, and it wasn't always smooth, but as we leaned into the process, we began to rebuild the trust and understanding that had been fractured.

One of the most profound realizations I had during this journey was that healing isn't linear. There were days when we took two steps forward and then one step back. There were times when old wounds resurfaced, bringing with them the temptation to fall back into old habits of resentment and anger. But each time that happened, I returned to prayer. I found myself asking not just for healing but for the strength to remain patient, for the wisdom to see beyond the surface of the conflict, and for the courage to keep showing up even when it felt difficult.

In these moments, I also began to understand the role of self-compassion in healing. I had been so focused on mending the relationship that I had neglected the importance of healing within myself. My faith reminded me that in order to truly heal in a relationship, we must first take care of our own hearts. I started to make space for my own healing, allowing myself to feel the emotions I had been suppressing, to grieve the hurts I had been holding onto, and to forgive myself for the mistakes I had made.

It wasn't just about forgiving my partner—it was about forgiving myself for the times I had been less than kind, for the moments when I had let my own pain dictate my actions. This self-forgiveness was perhaps one of the most challenging aspects of the healing process, but it was also one of the most liberating. As I allowed myself to heal, I became more capable of showing up fully in the relationship, with a heart that was open and ready to give and receive love without the heavy burden of unhealed wounds.

Healing in relationships, I've come to realize, is a continual process. It's not something that happens once and then it's done. It's an ongoing journey, one that requires attention, care, and a commitment to growth. Even now, after years of working through the challenges, I know that healing is something we must continually nurture. There will always be moments of misunderstanding, times when old wounds threaten to resurface, but with faith and the tools we've developed, we are better equipped to navigate those moments with grace and compassion.

One of the most beautiful outcomes of this journey has been the deepened sense of connection I now feel in my relationships. Healing has allowed us to move beyond the surface level, to create a bond that is rooted in honesty, vulnerability, and love. We've learned to communicate more openly, to listen without judgment, and to approach each other with a spirit of understanding rather than criticism. There is a sense of peace that comes from knowing that we can face challenges together, that we have the tools to heal and to grow stronger with each new obstacle.

As I reflect on this journey, I am filled with gratitude for the lessons I've learned along the way. Healing in relationships is not always easy, but it is one of the most transformative experiences we can have. It teaches us the value of patience, the importance of forgiveness, and the power of faith to mend even the deepest wounds. Through prayer, self-compassion, and a commitment to growth, I've discovered that healing is possible, even in the most challenging of circumstances.

Looking back, I can see that the hardships we faced were not obstacles to love but opportunities for growth. They pushed us to look deeper, to confront the parts of ourselves that needed healing, and to emerge on the other side with a stronger, more resilient bond. I now carry these lessons with me in all of my relationships, knowing that healing is not just about fixing what is broken but about creating space for love to flourish, even in the face of adversity.

Through this journey, I've come to understand that healing is a gift we give not only to each other but also to ourselves. It is a sacred process, one that requires faith, patience, and an open heart. And as we heal, we create the foundation for a relationship that is not only stronger but also more compassionate, more understanding, and more capable of weathering the storms that life inevitably brings.

Praying for Others in Conflict

The day I discovered the true power of praying for others in conflict was the day my world turned upside down. It wasn't a dramatic event or a life-altering tragedy, but rather a simple argument with my best friend, Sarah. We'd known each other since childhood, sharing countless secrets, dreams, and laughter. But on that fateful afternoon, a misunderstanding spiraled into harsh words and slammed doors. As I sat alone in my room, anger bubbling inside me, I felt an unexpected urge to pray - not for myself, but for Sarah.

Little did I know that this simple act would set me on a transformative journey, teaching me the profound impact of spiritual healing in relationships and how prayer can mend even the most fractured bonds?

At first, my prayer was awkward and stilted. I wasn't sure how to pray for someone I was angry with, someone who had hurt me. But as I continued, I felt a subtle shift within myself. The knot of anger in my chest began to loosen, and a sense of calm washed over me. I found myself genuinely wishing for Sarah's well-being, for her happiness, and for our friendship to heal.

This experience sparked a curiosity in me about the power of prayer in resolving conflicts and healing relationships. I began to explore this concept more deeply, both in my personal life and through conversations with others who had similar experiences.

One particularly enlightening conversation was with my neighbor, Mr. Johnson. I'd always known him as a kind, elderly gentleman who tended to his garden with meticulous care. One evening, as I was walking my dog past his house, I noticed him sitting on his porch with a troubled expression. Concerned, I stopped to chat.

Mr. Johnson shared that he was estranged from his son and hadn't spoken to him in years due to a bitter disagreement. The pain in his eyes was palpable as he spoke about missing his grandchildren and the regret that weighed heavily on his heart.

Without really thinking, I found myself sharing my recent experience with Sarah and how praying for her had helped me find peace. Mr. Johnson listened intently, a glimmer of hope appearing in his eyes. He confessed that he'd never considered praying for his son, always assuming that prayer was something you did for yourself or for those you loved unconditionally.

Inspired by our conversation, Mr. Johnson decided to give it a try. He promised to pray for his son every day for a month, focusing not on changing his son or the situation, but simply on sending love and positive energy.

Weeks passed, and I often saw Mr. Johnson on his porch, eyes closed in quiet contemplation. I wondered about his progress but didn't want to pry. Then, one sunny Saturday morning, I was surprised to see a car I didn't recognize parked in his driveway. As I walked closer, I saw Mr. Johnson embracing a younger man - his son - tears streaming down both their faces.

Later, Mr. Johnson shared with me that something extraordinary had happened. As he prayed for his son each day, he found his own heart softening. The anger and hurt he'd been holding onto for years began to dissipate, replaced by a genuine desire for reconciliation. Unbeknownst to him, his son had been going through a similar process, feeling an inexplicable urge to reach out and mend their relationship.

This experience with Mr. Johnson deepened my understanding of the power of praying for others in conflict. I realized that the act of prayer wasn't just about asking for divine intervention; it was a profound practice of empathy and compassion that could transform both the person praying and the person being prayed for.

Inspired by this realization, I decided to incorporate this practice more intentionally into my life. I began by making a list of all the relationships in my life that felt strained or broken. It was a longer list than I'd like to admit - old friends I'd drifted apart from, family members I struggled to understand, coworkers I found difficult to work with.

Each day, I committed to praying for one person on this list. I didn't pray for specific outcomes or for these people to change. Instead, I focused on sending them love, wishing for their happiness and well-being, and asking for guidance in how I might contribute to healing our relationship.

The results were subtle at first, but over time, I began to notice significant changes. In my prayers for my aunt, with whom I'd always had a tense relationship, I found myself remembering the times she'd been kind to me as a child. These memories softened my heart towards her, and the next time we met at a family gathering, I approached her with genuine warmth.

To my surprise, she responded in kind, and we had our first real conversation in years.

With a difficult coworker, my prayers helped me see beyond his abrasive exterior to the insecurities and pressures he might be facing. This new perspective allowed me to respond to his criticisms with patience and understanding, gradually transforming our interactions from confrontational to collaborative.

But perhaps the most profound change happened in my relationship with my younger sister, Emma. We'd always had a complicated relationship, marked by competition and misunderstanding. As the older sister, I often felt responsible for her, which translated into criticism and unsolicited advice. Emma, in turn, saw me as overbearing and judgmental.

When I began praying for Emma, I focused on seeing her through eyes of love and acceptance. I asked for the wisdom to understand her unique journey and the patience to support her without trying to control her path. As I prayed, I felt a deep sense of love and appreciation for her growing within me.

One evening, Emma called me in tears. She'd just gone through a difficult breakup and was feeling lost and alone. In the past, I might have jumped in with advice or even a lecture about her choices. But this time, influenced by weeks of praying for her, I simply listened. I held space for her pain without trying to fix it, and I expressed my unconditional love and support.

Emma later told me that this conversation was a turning point for her. She felt truly heard and accepted by me for the first time in years. From that day forward, our relationship began to heal and grow in ways I never thought possible.

As I continued this practice of praying for others in conflict, I began to see it as a form of active love. It wasn't passive or weak; it required strength and commitment. It challenged me to confront my own biases, fears, and shortcomings. Each prayer was an opportunity to grow in compassion and understanding.

I also discovered that this practice had a ripple effect. As I became more patient and understanding in my relationships, I noticed others around me doing the same. It was as if the energy of healing and reconciliation was contagious, spreading from one relationship to another.

One particularly powerful example of this ripple effect occurred in my workplace. I had been praying for my boss, Mr. Thompson, who was known for his harsh management style and high-stress demeanor. Rather than praying for him to change, I focused on understanding the pressures he might be under and sending him thoughts of peace and well-being.

Over time, I noticed subtle changes in our interactions. I felt more at ease in his presence, and he seemed to soften slightly in his approach to me. One day, after a particularly stressful meeting, Mr. Thompson surprised me by asking if everything was okay. He mentioned that he'd noticed a change in me recently - a calmness that he admired.

This opened the door to an honest conversation about workplace stress and the importance of supportive relationships. To my amazement, Mr. Thompson shared some of his own struggles and insecurities as a leader. This vulnerable exchange marked the beginning of a more positive and collaborative work environment, not just for me, but for our entire team.

As word spread about the changes in our department, other teams began to take notice. Soon, there was a company-wide initiative to improve workplace relationships and reduce stress. While I never mentioned my personal prayer practice, I knew in my heart that it had played a role in catalyzing this positive change.

Through these experiences, I came to understand that praying for others in conflict is not about trying to change them or the situation. It's about changing ourselves - our perceptions, our attitudes, and our capacity for love and understanding. As we open our hearts in prayer, we create space for healing and reconciliation to occur naturally.

I also learned that this kind of prayer requires patience and persistence. Some relationships took weeks or months to show signs of improvement. Others seemed to remain unchanged, at least on the surface. But I came to trust that even when I couldn't see the results, the act of praying was doing important work in my own heart and in the spiritual realm.

One relationship that tested this patience was with my childhood friend, Mark. We had drifted apart in our adult years due to differing lifestyles and values. Whenever we did interact, there was an underlying tension that made both of us uncomfortable. I began praying for Mark daily, focusing on the good memories we shared and wishing him well in his life journey.

Months passed without any apparent change. Then, out of the blue, I received a message from Mark. He was going through a tough time and remembered how I had always been a good listener. We met for coffee, and to my surprise, we fell into easy conversation, just like old times. The prayer had prepared my heart to receive him with openness and without judgment, allowing for a natural reconnection.

As my practice deepened, I began to see prayer as a form of spiritual energy that could transcend physical distance and even time. I started praying not just for current conflicts, but for past hurts and future challenges. I prayed for forgiveness - both to receive it and to give it. I prayed for the healing of generational wounds in my family line.

This expanded view of prayer led me to an unexpected insight about my relationship with my late grandfather. He had passed away when I was a teenager, and I had always carried a sense of guilt about our unresolved conflicts. One night, as I prayed, I felt a strong urge to direct my prayers towards him.

As I prayed for my grandfather, I felt a wave of love and understanding wash over me. I saw our conflicts from a new perspective, recognizing the generational patterns and societal pressures that had shaped his behavior. This spiritual experience brought a deep sense of peace and closure, healing a wound I had carried for years.

Throughout this journey, I've come to see prayer as a powerful tool for spiritual healing in relationships. It's not a magic solution that instantly resolves all conflicts, but rather a practice that gradually transforms our hearts and opens up new possibilities for connection and understanding.

I've learned that praying for others in conflict requires humility and a willingness to let go of our own need to be right. It asks us to see beyond the surface of conflicts to the shared humanity that unites us all. It challenges us to love unconditionally, even when it's difficult.

As I continue this practice, I'm constantly amazed by its power to heal and transform relationships. It has taught me that no conflict is truly insurmountable when approached with an open heart and a willingness to see the divine in every person.

To anyone struggling with conflict in their relationships, I would encourage you to try this practice of praying for those you're in conflict with. Start small if you need to - even a few moments of sincere prayer can begin to shift your perspective. Focus on sending love and positive energy rather than trying to change the other person or the situation.

Remember that the primary transformation happens within yourself. As you pray, pay attention to how your own feelings and attitudes begin to shift. Be patient with the process and trust that even when you can't see immediate results, your prayers are creating ripples of healing energy.

Most importantly, approach this practice with an open heart and a willingness to be surprised. Some of the most profound healings I've experienced have come in unexpected ways and from unexpected sources.

As I reflect on this journey, I'm filled with gratitude for the lessons I've learned and the healing I've experienced. Prayer has become not just a spiritual practice for me, but a way of life - a constant reminder to approach every interaction and every relationship with love, compassion, and an openness to divine guidance.

In a world often divided by conflict and misunderstanding, I believe that this practice of praying for others, especially those we're in conflict with, has the power to bring about profound healing and transformation. It reminds us of our fundamental interconnectedness and our shared capacity for love and forgiveness.

As we open our hearts in prayer, we create space for miracles to happen - not just in our personal relationships, but in our communities and in the world at large. And in doing so, we contribute to a larger healing that extends far beyond ourselves, touching lives in ways we may never fully know.

Restoring Trust through Prayer

Trust is one of the most fragile elements in any relationship, and I learned that lesson the hard way. I remember a time when I found myself standing at a crossroads, grappling with feelings of betrayal and disappointment. My heart felt heavy, and the weight of broken trust hung over me like a dark cloud. I desperately wanted to restore not just my faith in others but also my belief in myself. It was in that moment of vulnerability that I turned to prayer, seeking solace and a path toward healing.

The situation that prompted my quest for restoration began with a close friendship that I had cherished for years. We had shared countless memories, laughter, and secrets. I believed we were inseparable, bound by a deep connection. However, a misunderstanding spiraled into a conflict that shattered my sense of trust. Words were exchanged that cut deep, and the bond we had nurtured felt irreparably frayed. I remember sitting in my room, staring at the ceiling, feeling lost and alone. My heart ached not only for the friendship but also for my own sense of security.

In those moments of despair, I turned inward. I closed my eyes and began to pray. I felt the need to voice my pain, my confusion, and my desire for understanding. "Please," I whispered, "help me find the strength to forgive and the wisdom to rebuild." As I spoke, I felt the tears streaming down my cheeks, each one a release of the hurt I had carried for too long. I realized that prayer wasn't just a plea for help; it was a way to open my heart to the possibility of healing.

As days turned into weeks, I continued to engage in prayer. I set aside time each morning to reflect and connect with my inner self. I found comfort in words like "healing," "forgiveness," and "restoration." I visualized my heart mending, piece by piece, like a delicate tapestry being rewoven. In those quiet moments, I learned to listen, allowing the whispers of my spirit to guide me. I began to understand that restoring trust required patience—not just with others, but with myself.

During this process, I also sought to understand the other person's perspective. I realized that relationships are complex, and misunderstandings often stem from unmet expectations. In my prayers, I began to ask for clarity, not just for myself, but for my friend as well. I envisioned us sitting together, hearts open, ready to communicate honestly. This shift in perspective helped me cultivate empathy, an essential ingredient in rebuilding trust.

One evening, as I prayed, I felt an overwhelming sense of peace wash over me. I envisioned myself extending an olive branch, reaching out to my friend with love and understanding. I recognized that true restoration comes from a place of vulnerability, where one can express their feelings without fear of judgment. This realization inspired me to draft a message, one that conveyed my desire to reconnect and heal. I poured my heart into it, carefully choosing words that expressed both my hurt and my hope for reconciliation.

When I finally hit send, a wave of anxiety washed over me. What if my friend didn't respond? What if they felt the same way I did, harboring resentment and pain? Yet, amidst the uncertainty, I turned to prayer once more. I asked for courage, whatever the outcome might be. I reminded myself that I had taken a step toward healing, and that in itself was a victory.

Days passed, and I watched my phone, waiting for a response. In the silence, I felt my doubts creeping in. I turned to prayer again, asking for patience and trust in the process. I reminded myself that healing takes time and that not everything can be resolved immediately. I learned to breathe through the uncertainty, allowing myself to stay present in the moment instead of spiraling into anxiety about the future.

Then, one afternoon, I received a message back. My heart raced as I opened it. My friend expressed their own pain and confusion, acknowledging the misunderstanding that had caused our rift. They shared how much they valued our friendship and how deeply they regretted the words spoken in anger. In that moment, I felt a glimmer of hope. Our exchange became a bridge, allowing us to communicate openly and honestly about our feelings.

As we began to reconnect, I realized that prayer had not only helped me but had also opened a space for my friend to reflect on their own feelings. We decided to meet for coffee, and I approached the encounter with a sense of cautious optimism. I prayed before our meeting, asking for clarity and understanding. I wanted to listen more than I spoke, to truly hear what my friend had to say.

When we sat down, the initial awkwardness melted away as we shared stories and laughter, reminding ourselves of the bond we once had. We spoke about our feelings, the misunderstandings that had arisen, and the importance of trust in our friendship. I felt a sense of relief wash over me as we navigated this conversation with compassion. It became clear that we both desired healing and restoration.

One of the most powerful moments came when we talked about forgiveness. I expressed my struggle with trusting again, and my friend shared their own fears. We both acknowledged that rebuilding trust would take time. It wasn't a matter of simply saying "I forgive you" and moving on; it required ongoing commitment and understanding. We committed to being patient with each other and ourselves throughout the process.

As our friendship began to heal, I felt a profound shift within myself. The act of praying for restoration had opened my heart in ways I hadn't anticipated. I learned that prayer is not merely a request for assistance; it's an invitation to connect deeply with our own emotions and to seek understanding from others. It had become a tool for introspection, allowing me to confront my feelings and desires honestly.

In the following weeks, I continued to engage in prayer, but now it felt more like a conversation with an old friend. I would often express gratitude for the progress we were making, celebrating the small victories along the way. I found joy in the little moments—sharing a meal, laughing at inside jokes, and feeling the warmth of trust gradually returning.

However, I also recognized that the journey was not linear. There were moments when old wounds resurfaced, times when I felt the sting of betrayal all over again. In those instances, I turned to prayer, asking for strength to confront my feelings without letting them take over. I practiced self-compassion, reminding myself that healing is a process that requires time and patience.

One evening, I found myself reflecting on my journey while sitting in my favorite spot by the window. The sun set slowly, casting a warm glow across the room. I took a deep breath and began to pray, expressing gratitude for the lessons learned. I acknowledged the pain I had experienced, but I also celebrated the strength I discovered within myself. I realized that trust, once broken, can be rebuilt, but it requires vulnerability, openness, and a willingness to understand one another.

As our friendship deepened, I began to extend the principles of trust and prayer to other relationships in my life. I noticed how my perspective had shifted; I now approached conflicts with a sense of curiosity instead of defensiveness. I learned to engage in conversations with empathy, actively listening to others' viewpoints. This practice not only strengthened my relationships but also enriched my understanding of myself.

One day, while having a heart-to-heart with a family member, I found myself sharing my experiences of rebuilding trust. I spoke about the power of prayer in that journey and how it had guided me through the process. My family member listened intently, and I could see the wheels turning in their mind. They shared their own struggles with trust in a different context, and together we explored how prayer could be a source of strength for them as well.

In that moment, I recognized that my journey of restoring trust had become a catalyst for healing not only in my life but also in the lives of others. It felt as if my experience had created a ripple effect, encouraging those around me to confront their own challenges with grace and understanding. I began to understand that the act of sharing our stories can foster connection and empathy, creating a safe space for healing.

As I continued to pray and reflect, I also realized the importance of setting boundaries in my relationships. Trust is not just about forgiveness; it's also about understanding what is acceptable and what isn't. I learned to communicate my needs openly, ensuring that my relationships were built on mutual respect. This practice allowed me to feel empowered, knowing that I had a voice in my connections.

Looking back on my journey, I can see the profound impact that prayer has had on my ability to restore trust. It helped me navigate my emotions, embrace vulnerability, and foster genuine connections. I learned that trust is not an endpoint; it's a continuous process that requires ongoing effort and commitment. Each prayer became a stepping stone, guiding me through the ups and downs of relationships.

Now, I approach my relationships with a sense of hope and resilience. I understand that challenges will arise, but I also know that I have the tools to face them. I continue to pray, not just for myself but also for those I care about. I send out intentions for healing, understanding, and trust, knowing that each prayer contributes to a greater tapestry of connection.

In closing, I encourage you to explore the power of prayer in restoring trust within your own relationships. Embrace the journey of healing, allowing yourself to be vulnerable and open to understanding others. Remember that trust is built over time, and each step you take toward healing is a testament to your strength. Together, let us navigate the complexities of relationships with grace, fostering a deeper connection with ourselves and those we hold dear. Trust can be restored, and through prayer, we can mend the bonds that truly matter.

Prayers for Strengthening Relationships

I've always found that the strongest relationships don't just happen by chance. They are shaped, nurtured, and built upon a foundation that goes beyond mere connection. Yet, even with the deepest bonds, there come moments of strain, misunderstanding, or distance. It's in those moments that I've turned to prayer—not as a last resort but as a powerful source of guidance and strength. Prayer, for me, has been the invisible thread weaving us back together, reminding me of the importance of faith in relationships.

I remember a specific time when I felt the weight of a relationship that was slowly unraveling. We were close, once inseparable, but life had gotten in the way. The demands of work, family, and personal struggles pulled us in different directions, and without realizing it, we had drifted apart. There was no major argument, no dramatic falling out, just a slow and steady distancing. I kept telling myself that things would naturally go back to how they were, that the ebb and flow of life would bring us back to the center. But deep down, I knew that it wasn't something that could just "fix itself."

One evening, after a particularly long and frustrating day, I sat in silence and prayed. I didn't pray for the relationship to be instantly healed or for things to magically return to how they once were. Instead, I prayed for clarity, for the wisdom to see what was needed to rebuild that connection, and for the strength to take the necessary steps. That prayer wasn't just about the other person—it was about me, too. It was a request for the grace to let go of any resentment, to soften my heart, and to be open to rebuilding from a place of love and understanding.

As I sat there in the quiet, a memory came to me from years earlier. I had been in another challenging relationship, and at the time, I was full of frustration and confusion. A close friend had suggested that I start praying for the person every day, not just for resolution, but for their well-being, for their peace, and for their joy. It sounded simple, almost too simple to make a real difference, but I decided to try. Over time, I noticed a shift—not just in the relationship but in myself. My heart softened, and I became more patient, more compassionate, and more willing to communicate openly.

This memory reminded me of the power of prayer in relationships. It's not always about asking for things to be different but about seeking a deeper connection with the divine and allowing that connection to guide us in how we show up for each other. With this in mind, I began a new habit. Each day, I prayed for the relationship I was struggling with, not just in vague terms but specifically. I prayed for the person's happiness, for their growth, and for our ability to understand one another better. I prayed for patience, for the ability to listen without judgment, and for the courage to be vulnerable.

Slowly but surely, things began to change. The tension that had been building between us started to ease, and little by little, we reconnected. It wasn't an overnight transformation, but there was a noticeable shift in the way we interacted. I found myself more willing to reach out, to initiate conversations, and to express my feelings without fear of rejection or misunderstanding. Prayer had given me the strength to be open and honest, and it had created a space for healing.

I've seen this same dynamic play out in other relationships as well. There have been times when friends or family members were going through difficult seasons, and our connection suffered as a result. In the past, I might have taken it personally, feeling hurt or rejected when they pulled away. But through prayer, I've learned to approach those situations with a different mindset. Instead of reacting from a place of hurt or defensiveness, I now try to respond with empathy and understanding. I pray for them, for whatever challenges they are facing, and for the strength to support them in the ways they need most.

One such experience involved a close friend who had always been there for me. We had shared so many experiences together, from joyful celebrations to the toughest days of our lives. But out of nowhere, it seemed like she was retreating. Calls went unanswered, texts became short and distant, and I could sense that something was wrong. My first instinct was to feel hurt, to wonder what I had done wrong. But instead of letting those feelings fester, I turned to prayer.

In my prayers, I didn't ask for an immediate resolution. Instead, I asked for the grace to be patient, to not take her distance personally, and to trust that she was going through something that required space. I also prayed for her well-being, for whatever struggles she might be facing, and for our friendship to remain strong, even if it was quiet for a while. Over the following weeks, I found peace in the waiting. Prayer helped me see that not every silence is about me, that sometimes people need room to heal on their own terms.

Eventually, she reached out, and when she did, it became clear that she had been going through a deeply personal challenge that had nothing to do with me or our friendship. Because I had spent those weeks praying rather than stewing in my own insecurities, I was able to receive her with compassion and love. There was no resentment, no awkwardness—just a quiet understanding that our friendship had weathered another storm, not because we had talked through every detail, but because prayer had created a foundation of grace and trust.

I've also learned that prayer is essential when we're facing moments of conflict in relationships. There was a time when my partner and I were going through a particularly rough patch. We couldn't seem to agree on anything, and every conversation seemed to spiral into an argument. It felt like we were stuck in a cycle of frustration, with no clear way out. I knew that continuing down that path would only lead to more distance between us, but I wasn't sure how to break the pattern.

One evening, after another heated exchange, I felt this overwhelming need to turn to prayer. I prayed not for us to stop arguing or for one of us to suddenly "see the light." Instead, I prayed for understanding. I prayed for the ability to listen, really listen, to each other's perspectives. I asked for the wisdom to navigate our differences with love rather than frustration, and for the strength to stay committed to finding a resolution, even when it felt impossible.

Over the next few days, something shifted. The arguments didn't disappear overnight, but there was a noticeable change in how we approached them. We began to listen more intently, to speak with more kindness, and to stop trying to "win" the conversation. Prayer had softened our hearts, allowing us to see each other not as adversaries but as partners working through a difficult season together. That experience reminded me that prayer doesn't always change the external circumstances immediately, but it transforms how we show up in those circumstances.

Perhaps the most profound lesson I've learned about prayer in relationships is that it keeps us grounded in humility. In my prayers, I'm often reminded of my own shortcomings, of the ways I've fallen short in the relationship, and of the grace I need just as much as the other person. Prayer helps me let go of pride, of the need to be right, and of the desire to control the outcome. It brings me back to a place of surrender, where I can trust that the divine has a plan for the relationship, even if I can't see it clearly in the moment.

Through these experiences, I've come to see prayer as the lifeline that strengthens and sustains my relationships. It's not just a ritual or a practice —it's a conversation, a way of inviting the divine into the heart of my connections with others. When I pray for the people in my life, I'm not asking for perfection or for everything to go smoothly. I'm asking for the grace to navigate the inevitable challenges with love, patience, and understanding. I'm asking for the strength to show up fully, even when it's hard, and for the wisdom to see the other person through a lens of compassion rather than judgment.

As I look back on the relationships that have weathered storms, I can see the quiet but powerful role that prayer has played in each of them. It has helped me to stay anchored in love, to approach conflict with a spirit of humility, and to trust that healing is always possible, even when it feels far away. Prayer has taught me that relationships, like everything else in life, are a journey. They require care, attention, and a willingness to grow together through the ups and downs.

In the end, I've found that prayer doesn't just strengthen relationships—it transforms them. It deepens the bonds we share, not by erasing the challenges, but by giving us the strength to face them with grace. It reminds us that we are all imperfect, and that's okay. What matters is our willingness to keep trying, to keep loving, and to keep inviting the divine into the process of mending, healing, and strengthening the connections that mean the most to us. And through it all, prayer remains the quiet, steady force guiding us back to each other, time and time again.

Maintaining Healthy Relationships through Faith

I never expected a broken coffee mug to be the catalyst for transforming my relationships through faith. Yet there I stood, surrounded by ceramic shards, tears streaming down my face, realizing that something had to change. My marriage was crumbling, my friendships were strained, and I felt utterly alone. In that moment of despair, I heard a quiet whisper in my heart: "Pray." Little did I know that this simple prompt would lead me on a journey of spiritual healing, mending bonds not just in my marriage, but in all my relationships.

As I swept up the broken pieces of the mug, I began to pray. It wasn't an eloquent prayer by any means – just a desperate plea for help and guidance. But in that raw, vulnerable moment, I felt a spark of hope ignite within me. I realized that if I wanted my relationships to heal, I needed to approach them with a renewed sense of faith and purpose.

Over the next few months, I embarked on a journey to explore how faith could help maintain and heal my relationships. I started with my marriage, which had been strained by years of poor communication and unresolved conflicts. My husband, Tom, and I had grown distant, each of us retreating into our own worlds to avoid confrontation.

One evening, after another tense dinner filled with awkward silences, I suggested we try praying together. Tom looked skeptical but agreed to give it a shot. We sat on our living room couch, hands tentatively clasped, and I began to pray out loud. At first, it felt awkward and forced, but as I continued, pouring out my heart to God and asking for healing in our marriage, I felt the tension in the room start to dissipate.

To my surprise, Tom joined in, his voice soft but steady. He prayed for patience, for understanding, and for the strength to be a better partner. As we said "Amen," I opened my eyes to see tears in his. That night marked a turning point in our relationship. We didn't miraculously solve all our problems, but we had found a new way to connect and communicate.

We made praying together a nightly ritual, sharing our fears, hopes, and gratitude. Through these prayers, we began to see each other in a new light. I realized how much pressure Tom felt at work, and he understood my feelings of isolation as a stay-at-home mom. Our prayers became a safe space to voice our concerns and support each other.

As our connection deepened, we started to approach conflicts differently. Instead of immediately becoming defensive, we would pause and pray for guidance. This simple act often diffused tensions and helped us approach disagreements with more empathy and understanding.

One particularly challenging moment came when we disagreed about how to discipline our son, Jake. In the past, this would have led to a heated argument, but this time, we stopped and prayed together for wisdom. As we prayed, I felt a sense of calm wash over me, and I was able to listen to Tom's perspective with an open heart. We ended up finding a compromise that we both felt good about, and more importantly, we felt united as parents.

Encouraged by the positive changes in my marriage, I began to apply this faith-centered approach to other relationships in my life. I had a strained relationship with my sister, Sarah, stemming from childhood rivalries and perceived favoritism. We hadn't spoken in months, and the thought of reaching out filled me with anxiety.

One morning during my personal prayer time, I felt a strong urge to pray for Sarah. As I did, I found my heart softening towards her. I began to see our conflicts from a different perspective, recognizing the pain and insecurity that might be driving her actions. Over the next few weeks, I continued to pray for her daily, asking for healing in our relationship and for the courage to reach out.

Finally, I picked up the phone and called her. The conversation was awkward at first, but as we talked, I felt the walls between us start to crumble. I shared with her how I'd been praying for our relationship, and to my surprise, she confessed that she'd been doing the same. We both laughed and cried, marveling at how our individual faith journeys had led us back to each other.

From that day forward, Sarah and I made an effort to pray together regularly, even if it was just a quick phone call to share our intentions for the day. This practice helped us maintain our newfound connection and gave us a framework for addressing conflicts when they arose.

As I continued to explore the role of faith in maintaining healthy relationships, I realized that it wasn't just about praying for and with others. It was also about allowing my faith to shape my actions and attitudes in all my interactions. I began to approach my friendships with more intentionality, seeking to embody the love and compassion I believed in.

This shift in perspective was put to the test when my best friend, Lisa, went through a messy divorce. In the past, I might have jumped in with advice or criticism of her ex-husband. Instead, guided by my faith, I focused on being a compassionate listener and a source of support.

I prayed for Lisa daily, asking for strength and healing for her. When we met for coffee, instead of fueling her anger, I gently encouraged her to seek peace and forgiveness – not for her ex-husband's sake, but for her own healing. It wasn't always easy, and there were times when Lisa lashed out at me in her pain. But I held onto my faith, continuing to respond with love and patience.

Over time, I saw a change in Lisa. The bitterness that had consumed her began to fade, replaced by a quiet strength and resilience. She told me that my unwavering support and the prayers we shared had been a lifeline for her during the darkest times. Our friendship deepened through this experience, and I realized that by staying true to my faith, I had been able to be the friend she truly needed.

As I applied these principles to more of my relationships, I began to see a ripple effect in my community. At my son's school, I became known as someone who approached conflicts with calm and compassion. Other parents started coming to me for advice on how to handle disagreements with teachers or other parents.

I shared with them the importance of grounding ourselves in faith and prayer before approaching difficult conversations. I encouraged them to see the humanity in those they disagreed with and to seek understanding rather than just trying to prove their point.

One particularly challenging situation arose when there was a heated debate about changing the school curriculum. Parents were divided, and the atmosphere at PTA meetings became tense and hostile. Drawing on my faith, I suggested we start each meeting with a moment of silent reflection or prayer, inviting everyone to set their intentions for a productive and respectful discussion.

Initially, some parents were skeptical, but as we continued this practice, the tone of our meetings began to change. People became more willing to listen to opposing viewpoints, and we found common ground more easily. By the end of the school year, we had not only resolved the curriculum issue but had also formed a stronger, more cohesive parent community.

Through these experiences, I came to understand that maintaining healthy relationships through faith isn't about imposing my beliefs on others or using religion as a Band-Aid for deep-seated issues. Instead, it's about allowing my faith to transform me from the inside out, shaping how I approach every interaction and relationship in my life.

I learned the power of forgiveness, not as a one-time act, but as an ongoing practice. When a neighbor's dog destroyed my carefully tended garden, my first reaction was anger and a desire for retribution. But as I prayed about the situation, I felt challenged to respond with grace. I invited my neighbor over for tea, and we had an open conversation about the incident. Not only did she offer to help replant my garden, but we also formed a friendship that enriched both our lives.

This practice of faith-centered relationship maintenance also taught me the importance of boundaries. I had always struggled with saying no, often overcommitting myself out of a misguided sense of obligation. But as I deepened my faith, I realized that healthy relationships require healthy boundaries.

I started to view my time and energy as precious resources that I needed to steward wisely. This meant learning to say no to commitments that didn't align with my values or that would stretch me too thin. It wasn't easy, and I worried about disappointing people. But I found that when I explained my decisions prayerfully and respectfully, most people understood and respected my boundaries.

This new approach allowed me to be more fully present in the commitments I did make. When I volunteered at the local food bank, I wasn't distracted or resentful because I knew I was there by choice, aligned with my faith values. This led to deeper, more meaningful connections with my fellow volunteers and the people we served.

As my journey continued, I began to see every relationship as an opportunity for spiritual growth and healing. Even casual interactions with strangers became chances to practice kindness and compassion. I started to pray silently for the harried cashier at the grocery store or the frustrated driver who cut me off in traffic.

These small acts of faith-filled intention began to change how I moved through the world. I found myself more patient in long lines, more understanding of others' mistakes, and more quick to offer a smile or a kind word to those I encountered.

One day, while waiting in a long line at the post office, I struck up a conversation with the elderly woman behind me. As we chatted, she shared that she was sending a package to her estranged son, hoping to reconnect after years of silence. Moved by her story, I asked if I could pray with her right there in the line. She agreed, and we held hands, oblivious to the curious stares of others, as we prayed for reconciliation and healing in her family.

Weeks later, I ran into her again at the local park. With tears in her eyes, she told me that her son had called her after receiving the package. They had a long, heartfelt conversation and were taking steps to rebuild their relationship. She thanked me for the prayer we had shared, saying it had given her the courage to make that first move towards reconciliation.

This experience reinforced for me the power of bringing faith into every aspect of our lives, including our relationships with strangers. It showed me that we never know how a small act of faith might impact someone else's life in a profound way.

As I reflect on this journey of maintaining healthy relationships through faith, I'm struck by how much my life has changed. My marriage is stronger than ever, my family relationships have healed, and my friendships are deeper and more meaningful. But beyond these personal benefits, I've seen how this approach to relationships can create ripples of positive change in a community.

I've learned that faith-centered relationships require constant nurturing and attention. It's not always easy – there are still conflicts, misunderstandings, and hurt feelings. But I've found that when I approach these challenges with a foundation of faith, prayer, and intentionality, they become opportunities for growth rather than sources of division.

I've also discovered that this journey is ongoing. Each day brings new challenges and opportunities to apply these principles. Sometimes I falter, falling back into old patterns of reactivity or selfishness. But I've learned to be gentle with myself in these moments, to pray for strength and wisdom, and to keep trying.

To anyone struggling with their relationships, I would encourage you to explore how faith can be a healing and transformative force. Start small – perhaps with a daily prayer for a difficult relationship in your life. Be open to how this might change your perspective and actions. Remember that the goal isn't to change others, but to allow your faith to change you.

Cultivate practices that reinforce your faith in your daily interactions. This could be starting your day with a prayer of intention, pausing to take a deep breath and say a silent prayer before difficult conversations, or ending your day with gratitude for the relationships in your life.

Most importantly, be patient and persistent. Healing and maintaining relationships through faith is a lifelong journey. There will be setbacks and challenges, but each one is an opportunity for growth and deepening your faith.

As I continue on this path, I'm filled with gratitude for the ways in which faith has transformed my relationships and my life. I've learned that when we approach our connections with others from a place of faith, love, and intention, we open ourselves up to profound healing and joy. We create spaces where genuine understanding and compassion can flourish, and in doing so, we don't just improve our own lives – we contribute to healing the world around us, one relationship at a time.

THE LANGUAGE OF THE HEART: CRAFTING PERSONAL PRAYERS

Understanding the Personal Nature of Prayer

Prayer has always felt like a deeply personal journey for me, a sacred dialogue between my heart and the universe. I remember the first time I truly understood the power of prayer; it was a moment that shifted my perception forever. I was sitting alone on a park bench, feeling overwhelmed by life's demands. The noise of the city faded into the background as I closed my eyes and took a deep breath. In that stillness, I began to speak, not with formal words or rehearsed phrases, but simply with my heart. That experience marked the beginning of my understanding of prayer as a personal, intimate conversation—a language of the heart.

At that moment, I let go of the need for structure. I didn't craft elaborate sentences or worry about how my words would sound. Instead, I simply expressed my fears, hopes, and desires in a way that felt authentic to me. I asked for guidance in navigating the challenges ahead, and I felt a sense of relief wash over me as I poured my heart out. This was not about asking for things or seeking favors; it was about connecting with something greater than myself. It was in that space of vulnerability that I began to grasp the personal nature of prayer.

As I continued my journey, I found myself seeking prayer in various forms. I explored different traditions, reading about rituals and practices that resonated with me. However, I always returned to the understanding that prayer is unique to each individual. What works for one person might not work for another, and that's perfectly okay. I learned to embrace my own style, allowing my prayers to evolve based on my experiences and emotions.

One evening, I faced a particularly tough decision that left me feeling anxious and uncertain. I sat down on my living room floor with a journal in hand. I decided to write a letter to the universe—a prayer in written form. I poured out my thoughts, articulating my fears and hopes for the future. As I wrote, I felt an incredible sense of clarity emerging. Each word became a release, and I began to see the situation from a different perspective. I realized that prayer could also be a form of self-reflection, a way to process my thoughts and emotions.

After finishing my letter, I folded it carefully and placed it in a small box I kept on my desk. I decided to revisit it a month later, allowing the time to pass and the situation to unfold. This practice of writing my prayers became a cherished ritual, a way to document my spiritual journey. I learned that prayer is not just about immediate answers; it's about cultivating trust in the process of life.

In the weeks that followed, I continued this practice, allowing my letters to become a sacred space for my thoughts. I would sit quietly, reflecting on my day, and let my heart guide my pen. I found that writing helped me articulate my feelings more clearly than I could in spoken prayer. I could take my time, crafting each sentence with care, pouring my soul onto the page. This process deepened my connection to my own emotions and allowed me to explore the intricacies of my heart.

One day, while writing, I felt particularly inspired to express gratitude. I began listing the things I appreciated in my life—my supportive friends, the beauty of nature, even the challenges that had helped me grow. As I wrote, I felt a shift within me. Gratitude became a prayer in itself, a way to acknowledge the abundance surrounding me. I learned that gratitude is a powerful form of prayer, one that opens the heart and invites positivity into our lives.

This realization led me to another profound understanding—the importance of balance in prayer. I noticed that my conversations with the universe often leaned heavily on requests for help or guidance. So, I made a conscious effort to incorporate gratitude into my daily prayers. Each morning, I would start by acknowledging the blessings I had, no matter how small. This practice transformed my perspective, allowing me to approach each day with a sense of appreciation rather than anxiety.

As my relationship with prayer deepened, I began to experiment with different environments. I found that the setting in which I prayed significantly influenced my experience. Some days, I would head to the park, surrounded by the tranquility of nature. Other times, I would light a candle in my room, creating a cozy atmosphere that invited reflection. I learned that the space around us can enhance our connection to prayer, making it feel more intimate and personal.

One chilly autumn afternoon, I took a long walk through a nearby forest. The crisp air invigorated me, and the vibrant colors of the leaves filled me with awe. I found a quiet spot beside a babbling brook and decided to sit and pray. I closed my eyes and listened to the sounds of water flowing over rocks, the rustling of leaves, and the distant chirping of birds. In that serene environment, my heart opened even wider. I spoke my thoughts aloud, letting them drift away like the leaves falling from the trees. Nature became a backdrop for my prayer, reminding me of the beauty and interconnectedness of all things.

During this time, I also began to notice how my prayers impacted my relationships. I found myself praying for my loved ones, asking for their happiness and well-being. I realized that prayer could extend beyond my own needs and desires. It became a way to cultivate compassion and connection with those around me. I felt a sense of responsibility to hold space for my friends and family, to lift them up in my thoughts and intentions.

One evening, a dear friend confided in me about a difficult situation they were facing. I listened, offering support and understanding. After our conversation, I felt compelled to pray for them. I took a moment to sit quietly, visualizing my friend surrounded by love and light. I asked for guidance and strength to help them navigate their challenges. This simple act of prayer became a source of comfort for both of us. My friend later shared how much it meant to them to know I was holding them in my thoughts.

As I continued to engage in this practice, I discovered that prayer could also be a source of healing. I encountered moments of grief and loss, times when the weight of sorrow felt almost unbearable. In those dark hours, I turned to prayer for solace. I learned to express my pain without reservation, allowing myself to grieve openly. I remember one particularly difficult night, sitting on my bed with tears streaming down my face. I spoke to the universe, pouring out my heart in raw honesty. In that moment, I felt an overwhelming sense of release. It was as if my pain had transformed into a prayer, a way to honor my feelings while seeking comfort.

Through this process, I came to understand that prayer doesn't always have to be about finding answers or solutions. Sometimes, it's about simply being present with our emotions. I learned to embrace the moments of uncertainty and fear, allowing them to coexist with my desire for healing. This realization became a profound aspect of my spiritual journey, teaching me that vulnerability is a strength, not a weakness.

As time passed, my understanding of prayer continued to deepen. I began to explore the concept of intention-setting—another layer to the personal nature of prayer. I learned that when I approached prayer with clear intentions, I could cultivate a sense of purpose and direction. Each intention became a guiding light, illuminating my path as I navigated life's complexities.

One evening, I decided to create a vision board, a visual representation of my intentions for the coming year. I gathered magazines, scissors, and glue, excited to bring my dreams into focus. As I cut out images and words that resonated with me, I reflected on the desires that filled my heart. I prayed over each intention, infusing them with love and hope. This creative process became a powerful form of prayer, allowing me to articulate my aspirations while connecting with my inner self.

In the following months, I revisited my vision board regularly, reinforcing my intentions through prayer. I learned to celebrate each small step I took toward my goals, recognizing that progress doesn't always look the same. Some days, I stumbled, and other days, I soared. But through it all, I remained anchored in my practice of prayer. It became a source of strength and clarity, guiding me through both triumphs and challenges.

One of the most profound lessons I learned about the personal nature of prayer is that it's not confined to any specific form or structure. It's an ever-evolving conversation that reflects our unique experiences and beliefs. I began to embrace spontaneity in my prayers, letting them flow naturally without rigid expectations. Some days, I would sing my prayers, allowing my voice to rise in joyful expression. Other times, I would meditate in silence, letting my thoughts wander freely.

This flexibility allowed me to connect with my spirituality in new and unexpected ways. I discovered that prayer could be woven into the fabric of my daily life. I began to pray while cooking, expressing gratitude for the nourishment I was preparing. I would whisper prayers during my morning commute, finding moments of connection amidst the hustle and bustle of the day. I realized that prayer doesn't have to be confined to a specific time or place; it can be a continuous thread that runs through our lives.

As I embraced this personal approach to prayer, I also began to explore the concept of community prayer. I found joy in coming together with others to share our intentions and support one another. I attended small gatherings where we would sit in a circle, each person taking turns sharing their prayers and aspirations. In those moments, I felt a deep sense of connection, knowing that we were all lifting each other up in love and light. These experiences reinforced my understanding that prayer can be both personal and communal, a beautiful tapestry woven from individual threads.

Through all these experiences, I've come to see prayer as a dynamic journey—a language of the heart that evolves with us. It allows us to express our deepest emotions, seek guidance, and celebrate the beauty of life. I've learned that there's no right or wrong way to pray; what matters most is the intention and authenticity behind it.

Now, as I sit in quiet reflection, I feel immense gratitude for the personal nature of prayer in my life. It has become a cherished practice, a source of comfort, and a guiding light. I have learned to approach each prayer with an open heart, embracing the journey with all its complexities. I invite you to explore your own relationship with prayer, to discover the language of your heart, and to craft personal prayers that resonate deeply within you. In this sacred dialogue, you may find the connection and healing you've been seeking, allowing your spirit to soar in the process.

Techniques for Writing Your Own Prayers

The first time I sat down to write my own prayer, I felt uncertain, like I was stepping into unfamiliar territory. I had always thought of prayer as something prescribed, something ancient and already written for me to follow. But in that moment, I realized that prayer could be so much more. It didn't have to be scripted or rehearsed. It could be a conversation, a deeply personal exchange between me and the divine, shaped by my own heart and circumstances.

I was going through a particularly tough time, one of those moments where life seems to hit from all sides. I felt overwhelmed, weighed down by emotions I didn't know how to express. The prayers I had been saying, the ones I had recited countless times before, felt distant—like they didn't quite match what I was experiencing. So, on a quiet afternoon, I decided to try something different. I sat with a blank page in front of me, a pen in my hand, and I began to write.

At first, it felt a bit strange, almost like I was journaling instead of praying. But as I wrote, the words started to flow, and I realized that I was pouring out my heart in a way that felt incredibly natural. I wasn't worrying about saying the "right" thing or following any kind of format. I was simply expressing what I was feeling in that moment, with honesty and vulnerability. That was the first lesson I learned about writing my own prayers: authenticity matters more than anything else.

I remember starting with gratitude, even though I wasn't in the best of moods. I found that beginning with gratitude grounded me, reminded me of the good things in my life, even when I was struggling. I wrote about the small blessings that were easy to overlook—the quiet moments of peace, the support of loved ones, the beauty of nature. Gratitude softened my heart and opened me up to a deeper connection. It's something I now include in every prayer I write, no matter what's going on in my life. Gratitude, for me, is like the doorway to divine presence.

One technique that has helped me immensely is to focus on simplicity. At first, I thought that my prayers needed to be poetic or profound to "count." But I quickly learned that the most powerful prayers are often the simplest. One evening, after a particularly stressful day, I found myself writing just a few sentences: "I'm tired. I don't know what to do next. Please help me find some peace." That prayer, though short, was incredibly meaningful. It captured exactly how I was feeling, and in that moment, I felt heard. Sometimes, a prayer can be as simple as asking for strength or clarity, and that's enough.

Another important aspect of writing my own prayers has been learning to let go of perfection. In the early days, I would often stop and rewrite my words, trying to make them sound more "proper" or polished. But the more I practiced, the more I realized that perfection isn't the point. The divine isn't grading my grammar or my phrasing. What matters is the sincerity behind the words. Now, when I write, I focus on letting the words come as they are, without overthinking or editing too much. Prayer is an expression of the heart, and the heart isn't always neat and tidy. Sometimes it's messy, and that's okay.

There was a time when I was dealing with a difficult relationship, one that seemed to be filled with misunderstandings and unresolved hurt. I felt stuck, unsure of how to heal the divide. So, I sat down and began writing a prayer about the situation. At first, it was hard to find the right words, but then I started by acknowledging the pain and confusion I was feeling. I didn't sugarcoat it. I let the rawness of my emotions come through, writing about my frustration and sadness. Then, I asked for guidance, for the wisdom to know how to move forward and the grace to approach the relationship with love and forgiveness.

That prayer became a turning point for me. By writing it, I was able to release some of the tension I had been holding onto, and I felt a sense of peace wash over me. Writing prayers has become a way for me to process difficult emotions, to name what's going on inside of me, and to seek divine support in navigating those challenges. There's something powerful about putting pen to paper and seeing my emotions reflected back at me. It helps me clarify what I'm really feeling and what I need in that moment.

As I've continued to write my own prayers, I've also discovered the importance of listening. Prayer, for me, isn't just about speaking—it's about creating space for divine wisdom to speak back. Often, after I've finished writing, I'll sit in silence for a few moments, letting the words settle. In that quiet, I've found answers I wasn't expecting, subtle nudges or insights that seem to come from a place beyond my own understanding. Prayer, I've learned, is a dialogue, not a monologue. Writing down my prayers allows me to express my side of the conversation, but the real magic happens when I pause to listen for the divine response.

One of the most transformative experiences I had with writing my own prayers came during a time of uncertainty in my career. I was at a crossroads, unsure of which direction to take. I had been praying for clarity, but nothing seemed to be shifting. So, one day, I decided to write down my fears and doubts. I didn't hold back—I wrote about my anxieties, my sense of failure, and my frustration with the lack of clear direction. But as I continued to write, something shifted. The tone of my prayer changed. I began to write about my desire for purpose and meaning, for the courage to take risks, and for the faith to trust in the unknown.

By the time I finished, I felt a sense of relief. I had named my fears, but I had also named my hopes. That prayer became a declaration of trust, a way of affirming that even though I didn't have all the answers, I believed that something greater was guiding me. In the weeks that followed, opportunities started to unfold in ways I hadn't anticipated. Writing that prayer helped me shift from a place of fear to a place of trust, and it reminded me that sometimes the act of writing can be a way of manifesting what we need most.

One thing that has become central to my practice of writing prayers is the idea of intention. I've learned to approach prayer not just as a request for help or intervention, but as a way of setting an intention for my own growth and transformation. For example, when I'm feeling overwhelmed by stress, I'll write a prayer not just asking for peace, but expressing my intention to cultivate more peace in my life. I'll write about the ways I want to create space for rest, to let go of unnecessary worries, and to find balance in my day-to-day life. Writing prayers in this way has made them feel more empowering, as though I'm co-creating with the divine rather than passively waiting for something to change.

There's also something deeply personal about writing prayers that reflect my own spiritual journey. When I write, I don't feel the need to conform to any particular style or tradition. My prayers are uniquely mine, shaped by my experiences, my beliefs, and my relationship with the divine. Some days, my prayers are filled with gratitude and joy, and other days, they're full of questions and uncertainty. But each one is an honest reflection of where I am in that moment. Writing my own prayers has allowed me to develop a more intimate and authentic connection with my spirituality.

One technique that has been especially helpful is using imagery in my prayers. Sometimes, when words alone don't seem to capture what I'm feeling, I'll use metaphors or visual language to express my emotions. For example, when I'm feeling overwhelmed, I might write about the sensation of being caught in a storm and ask for the strength to weather it. When I'm feeling lost, I might write about walking through a fog and ask for the light to guide me. These images help me tap into a deeper level of meaning and emotion, and they make my prayers feel more vivid and alive.

Writing my own prayers has become a practice of self-discovery as much as it's a spiritual practice. It's a way of checking in with myself, of asking, "What do I need right now?" and "How can I invite the divine into this moment?" It's also a way of celebrating the ordinary moments of life, of pausing to acknowledge the beauty and the blessings that are so easy to overlook. I've written prayers about the simple joys of a quiet morning, the peace that comes from a walk in nature, and the warmth of connection with loved ones. Writing these prayers has helped me cultivate a deeper sense of gratitude and presence in my daily life.

I've also found that writing prayers can be a way of offering support to others. When a friend or family member is going through a difficult time, I'll often write a prayer for them. It's my way of holding them in my heart, of sending love and light their way, even if I can't be with them physically. Writing these prayers helps me feel connected to the people I care about, and it's a reminder that we are all linked in this web of life, supporting and uplifting one another through our thoughts and intentions.

Ultimately, writing my own prayers has transformed the way I approach spirituality. It has given me a sense of agency in my relationship with the divine, a way of actively participating in my own healing and growth. It's a practice that has brought me clarity in times of confusion, peace in times of turmoil, and joy in times of celebration. Each prayer I write is a reflection of my journey, a snapshot of where I am in that moment. And through it all, I've learned that prayer isn't about perfection or formality—it's about speaking the language of the heart.

Finding Words for Unspoken Emotions

The day I realized I couldn't pray was the day my world shattered. I stood in the quiet of my bedroom, eyes closed, hands clasped, but the words wouldn't come. How could I speak to a God I wasn't sure I believed in anymore? How could I express the turmoil in my heart when I couldn't even understand it myself? Little did I know, this moment of silence would be the beginning of a profound journey into the language of the heart and the art of crafting personal prayers?

I've always been a words person. As a writer, I prided myself on my ability to articulate complex thoughts and emotions. But in the face of personal tragedy – the unexpected loss of my younger brother – words failed me. The prayers that once flowed easily now felt hollow and inadequate. I found myself struggling not just with grief, but with a crisis of faith that left me feeling lost and alone.

In the weeks that followed, I went through the motions of my daily life, but inside, I was screaming. How could I express this pain? How could I find comfort in prayer when the very act felt like a betrayal of my doubts? I needed a new language, one that could bridge the gap between my broken heart and the divine.

My journey began with silence. Unable to form coherent prayers, I started sitting in quiet meditation each morning. At first, it felt awkward and unproductive. My mind raced with unspoken words and unanswered questions. But as days turned into weeks, I began to find comfort in the stillness. In the absence of words, I started to hear the whispers of my heart.

One morning, as I sat in my usual spot by the window, watching the sunrise paint the sky in hues of pink and gold, I felt an overwhelming surge of emotion. Without thinking, I grabbed a notebook and began to write. What flowed onto the page wasn't a traditional prayer, but a raw, unfiltered outpouring of my soul:

"God, or Universe, or whatever you are – I'm angry. I'm hurting. I don't understand why this happened. I want to believe you're there, but I can't feel you. Help me find my way back to you."

As I wrote those words, tears streamed down my face. For the first time since my brother's death, I felt a release. It wasn't eloquent or poetic, but it was real. I realized that this – this messy, honest expression – was a form of prayer. It was the beginning of my journey into crafting personal prayers that truly reflected the language of my heart.

Encouraged by this breakthrough, I began to explore different ways of expressing my innermost thoughts and feelings to the divine. I experimented with various forms of creative expression, allowing each to become a unique form of prayer.

One day, frustrated with my inability to verbalize my emotions, I turned to art. I spread a large canvas on the floor and began to paint with my hands, letting colors and shapes flow freely. As I worked, I found myself having an internal dialogue with God. Each stroke of color became a wordless prayer, expressing what I couldn't say aloud. The resulting abstract painting became a visual representation of my spiritual journey – chaotic, colorful, and deeply personal.

Another time, feeling overwhelmed by the weight of my grief, I went for a walk in the woods near my home. As I moved through the trees, I began to collect small objects – a smooth stone, a fallen leaf, a twig. Each item I picked up became a tangible prayer, a physical representation of my hopes, fears, and questions. I arranged these objects in a small circle on the forest floor, creating a sort of natural altar. Standing there, surrounded by the quiet strength of the trees, I felt a profound sense of connection to something greater than myself.

These nontraditional forms of prayer opened up new avenues for me to explore my spirituality. I began to see prayer not as a rigid, formulaic practice, but as a fluid, creative act of communication with the divine. This shift in perspective allowed me to approach prayer with a sense of curiosity and openness, rather than obligation or doubt.

As I continued to experiment with different forms of personal prayer, I found that music became a powerful medium for expressing my deepest emotions. Though I'm not a skilled musician, I began to play simple melodies on an old guitar, allowing the music to become a form of prayer. Sometimes I would sing, other times I would simply let the instrument speak for me. The resonance of the strings seemed to vibrate with the longings of my soul, creating a harmony between my inner world and the divine.

One particularly difficult evening, overwhelmed by memories of my brother, I picked up the guitar and began to strum. Without conscious thought, a melody emerged, accompanied by words that seemed to come from somewhere beyond me:

"In the silence of my sorrow,

In the spaces between breaths,

I'm reaching out to find you,

In life, in love, in death."

As I sang these words over and over, I felt a profound sense of peace wash over me. It wasn't a resolution to my grief or doubts, but a moment of connection – to my brother's memory, to my own heart, and to something greater than myself. This improvised song became a personal prayer that I returned to often, a musical touchstone in times of emotional turbulence.

As my practice of crafting personal prayers deepened, I began to notice a shift in how I perceived the world around me. Everyday moments became opportunities for connection and reflection. The sight of a butterfly emerging from its chrysalis became a prayer for transformation. The sound of rain on the roof turned into a meditation on cleansing and renewal. I started to see the sacred in the ordinary, and my prayers began to reflect this newfound awareness.

One morning, as I prepared my usual cup of coffee, I was struck by the rich aroma and the warmth of the mug in my hands. In that moment, this simple act became a prayer of gratitude:

"Divine Creator, thank you for this moment of warmth and comfort. As this coffee nourishes my body, May your love nourish my soul. In each sip, remind me of the richness of life and the blessings that surround me, even in times of sorrow."

This practice of finding prayer in everyday moments helped me to stay connected to my spirituality throughout the day, not just during designated prayer times. It became a way of living prayerfully, of seeing the divine in the mundane.

As I continued to explore this new way of praying, I found that my prayers began to change in tone and content. Instead of asking for specific outcomes or answers, I found myself praying for openness, understanding, and strength. My prayers became less about changing external circumstances and more about transforming my own heart and perspective.

One significant shift came when I started incorporating forgiveness into my personal prayers. I realized that I had been harboring anger – at God, at the universe, at myself – for my brother's death. This anger was a heavy burden, one that was hindering my healing process. I decided to create a ritual of forgiveness as a form of prayer.

I wrote down all the things I was angry about on small pieces of paper. Then, one by one, I read each aloud, allowing myself to fully feel the emotion associated with it. After reading each one, I would say, "I release this anger. I choose forgiveness." Then I would burn the paper, watching the smoke rise as a symbol of letting go.

This ritual became a powerful form of prayer for me. It wasn't easy – some days, the words of forgiveness felt hollow, and I had to repeat the ritual multiple times before I felt a true release. But over time, I found that this practice of intentional forgiveness prayer began to lighten the load of grief I carried.

As I became more comfortable with this new, personal approach to prayer, I began to share my experiences with others. I started a small group in my community for people who were struggling with traditional forms of prayer.

We met weekly to explore different creative prayer practices and to support each other in our spiritual journeys.

In this group, I witnessed the transformative power of personal prayer in others' lives. One woman, who had been estranged from her faith after a painful divorce, found healing through writing letters to God. Another member discovered a deep connection to the divine through dance, expressing his prayers through movement when words failed him.

Leading this group taught me that there is no one-size-fits-all approach to prayer. Each person's journey is unique, and the language of the heart speaks in many dialects. This realization helped me to embrace the evolving nature of my own prayer life, understanding that it would continue to change and grow as I did.

As my practice of crafting personal prayers deepened, I found that it began to influence other areas of my life. My writing took on a new depth and authenticity as I learned to tap into the raw, honest voice I had discovered in my prayers. My relationships improved as I became more attuned to the unspoken emotions of others and more willing to express my own.

One particularly powerful moment came during a difficult conversation with my parents. We had been struggling to connect in the aftermath of my brother's death, each of us locked in our private grief. As we sat together, the weight of unspoken words hanging heavy between us, I felt prompted to share one of my personal prayers.

With a shaky voice, I began to recite a poem-prayer I had written:

"In this space between us,

Where words cannot reach,

Let love flow like a river,

Healing what we cannot speak."

As I spoke these words, I saw tears form in my mother's eyes. My father reached out and took my hand. In that moment, my personal prayer became a bridge, connecting us in our shared pain and love. It opened a door for us to begin talking about our grief and to support each other in our healing process.

This experience showed me the power of vulnerable, authentic prayer to foster connection not just with the divine, but with those around us. I began to see how the practice of crafting personal prayers could be a tool for building community and fostering understanding.

As my journey continued, I found that my prayers began to extend beyond my personal concerns. As I healed and grew, I felt called to pray for others and for the world at large. But rather than resorting to generic, catch-all phrases, I sought to craft prayers that were specific and heartfelt.

When a friend was going through a difficult time, instead of simply saying "I'll pray for you," I took the time to write a personalized prayer-poem for her. I incorporated details of her situation and personality, making it a unique expression of care and support. This practice of crafting individualized prayers for others became a way for me to deepen my connections and to put my empathy into action.

I also began to engage with global issues through prayer, but in a more personal and creative way. When I felt overwhelmed by news of environmental destruction, instead of feeling helpless, I would go out into nature and create environmental prayer-art. I would arrange leaves, stones, and flowers into mandalas, each element representing a specific prayer for healing and protection of our planet.

This evolution in my prayer life taught me that personal, heartfelt prayer could be a powerful force for change – both within myself and in the world around me. It wasn't about expecting miraculous interventions, but about aligning my heart and actions with my deepest values and hopes.

As I reflect on this journey of finding words for unspoken emotions and crafting personal prayers, I'm struck by how far I've come from that moment of silent despair in my bedroom. Prayer, which once felt like an insurmountable barrier, has become a source of comfort, creativity, and connection in my life.

I've learned that the language of the heart is rich and varied. It speaks not just in words, but in colors, sounds, movements, and silences. Crafting personal prayers is not about finding the right words to say, but about creating authentic expressions of our innermost selves.

This journey has taught me that prayer is not a one-way communication, but a dialogue. It's not just about speaking, but also about listening – to our own hearts, to the world around us, and to the whispers of the divine. Sometimes, the most powerful prayers are the ones we don't speak at all, but live out in our actions and attitudes.

I've also discovered that prayer is not a static practice, but one that grows and changes with us. What sustains us in one season of life may not serve us in another. The beauty of personal prayer is its flexibility – its ability to adapt to our changing needs, doubts, and discoveries.

For those who find themselves struggling with traditional forms of prayer, or who feel disconnected from their spirituality, I offer this encouragement: don't be afraid to explore, to experiment, to find your own unique way of connecting with the divine. Your prayers don't need to look or sound like anyone else's. They only need to be authentic expressions of your heart.

Start small. Pay attention to the moments that move you – a beautiful sunset, a child's laughter, a moment of unexpected kindness. Let these become seeds for your prayers. Use whatever medium speaks to you – words, art, music, movement, or simply your breath. Trust that your sincere desire to connect is itself a form of prayer.

Remember that crafting personal prayers is a practice. Like any skill, it takes time to develop. Be patient with yourself. Embrace the awkwardness, the uncertainty, the moments when words fail you. These too are part of the journey.

Most importantly, don't judge your prayers. There is no right or wrong way to express the language of your heart. Your doubts, your anger, your confusion – all of these have a place in your prayers. The divine can handle your raw, unfiltered emotions. In fact, I've found that it's in these moments of brutal honesty that the most profound connections occur.

As I continue on this path of crafting personal prayers, I'm filled with a sense of wonder and gratitude. Each day brings new opportunities to explore the language of my heart, to deepen my connection with the divine, and to express the inexpressible.

I've come to see prayer not as a duty or a desperate plea for help, but as a creative act of love – love for myself, for others, for the world, and for the mystery that underlies it all. It's a continual process of opening my heart, of paying attention, of seeking connection.

In the end, I've found that the most powerful prayer is often the simplest: showing up, being present, and opening ourselves to the possibility of connection. Whether through words, art, music, or silence, when we offer our true selves in prayer, we participate in a beautiful, ongoing conversation with the divine.

So to anyone struggling to find words for their unspoken emotions, I say: listen to the language of your heart. It's speaking all the time, in whispers and in roars. Your task is simply to pay attention, to honor what you hear, and to let it guide you in crafting prayers that are uniquely, authentically yours. In doing so, you may find not just a new way to pray, but a new way to live – with greater awareness, deeper connection, and a renewed sense of wonder at the sacred that surrounds us always.

Using Prayer Journals for Spiritual Growth

I never imagined that a simple notebook could become a vessel for my spiritual growth, but that's precisely what happened when I started using a prayer journal. It all began on a rainy afternoon when I felt particularly restless. The weight of the world seemed to press down on me, and I craved a way to connect more deeply with my thoughts and emotions. I stumbled upon an old, unused journal tucked away on my bookshelf, its pages blank and waiting for my words. Little did I know, this would spark a transformative journey—a journey of self-discovery, reflection, and deepening faith.

As I opened that journal for the first time, I felt both excitement and apprehension. The blank pages beckoned me, inviting me to pour out my heart. I picked up a pen and started writing. At first, I simply expressed my thoughts: my worries about work, my hopes for the future, and my gratitude for the small joys in life. I found myself writing as if I were having a conversation with a close friend. This intimate setting allowed me to be honest and vulnerable, paving the way for deeper spiritual exploration.

In those early entries, I discovered the cathartic power of writing. I would often start by writing a short prayer, asking for guidance or clarity on specific issues. For instance, one day, I felt particularly anxious about a big decision regarding my career. I wrote, "Please help me find the courage to make the right choice." As I continued to write, I found that my thoughts began to flow more freely. I recorded my fears and my aspirations, exploring the depths of my heart. I realized that this process was not just about asking for help; it became a way to understand myself better.

As I continued to use my prayer journal, I noticed a significant shift in my perspective. The more I wrote, the more I learned to listen to my inner voice. I began to ask myself deeper questions: What do I truly want? What fears hold me back? Each entry became an opportunity for reflection, a chance to peel back the layers of my thoughts and emotions. I found that the act of writing was like holding a mirror to my soul, revealing truths I had long ignored.

One particularly enlightening moment came after I wrote about a painful experience from my past. I had been holding onto resentment for a long time, and it weighed heavily on my heart. In my journal, I wrote about the incident in detail, exploring my feelings of hurt and betrayal. As I poured out my emotions onto the page, I began to feel lighter, as if I was releasing a burden I had carried for too long. I closed my entry with a prayer for forgiveness, not just for the other person but for myself as well. That entry marked a turning point in my healing process, a moment of clarity that opened the door to greater compassion.

The beauty of a prayer journal lies in its ability to capture the ebb and flow of our spiritual journeys. I found myself returning to past entries, reflecting on how far I had come. I would often read through my earlier prayers, marveling at the ways in which my thoughts and intentions had evolved. This practice of revisiting my writings helped me appreciate the progress I had made. It reminded me that spiritual growth is not always linear; it often unfolds in unexpected ways.

One day, I decided to create a section in my journal dedicated solely to gratitude. I titled it "Grateful Heart" and committed to writing down at least three things I was grateful for each day. This simple act transformed my perspective. I started noticing the small moments—the warmth of the sun on my skin, the laughter of a friend, the comfort of a good book. By acknowledging these blessings, I cultivated a deeper sense of appreciation for life itself. Each entry became a joyous celebration, an acknowledgment of the beauty that surrounded me.

As I filled my journal with prayers and reflections, I also began to explore the concept of intention-setting. I realized that prayer could be a powerful tool for manifesting my desires. One evening, I sat down and wrote out my intentions for the upcoming month. I focused on specific areas of my life where I sought growth—my relationships, my career, and my personal development. I crafted each intention with care, infusing it with love and hope. This practice became a way for me to align my actions with my goals, creating a roadmap for my spiritual journey.

I also discovered the power of visualization through my prayer journal. I began to incorporate visual elements into my entries. I would cut out images from magazines that resonated with my intentions and paste them alongside my written prayers. This creative aspect added another layer to my practice, allowing me to engage with my goals on a deeper level. Each time I opened my journal, I was inspired by the visuals, reminding me of the dreams I was nurturing.

As I continued to explore the depths of my heart through journaling, I found that my prayers evolved as well. They became more personal, more intimate. I started addressing my prayers with a sense of warmth and familiarity. Instead of a formal "Dear God," I might begin with "Hey there, Universe," or "My dear Heart." This shift felt liberating; it allowed me to express my spiritual connection in a way that felt authentic to me. I learned that prayer doesn't have to follow a specific format; it can be a reflection of our unique relationship with the divine.

One evening, I found myself grappling with feelings of doubt and uncertainty. Life had thrown a few curveballs my way, and I felt lost. I opened my journal and began to write about my fears. I wrote about my worries regarding my career, my relationships, and my future. As I expressed my concerns, I felt a wave of vulnerability wash over me. I allowed myself to be honest, to confront the fears that had been lurking in the shadows.

In that moment of raw honesty, I paused and took a few deep breaths. I realized that I needed to reframe my doubts into prayers. I began to rewrite my fears as affirmations. Instead of "What if I fail?" I transformed it into "I trust that I am capable of overcoming challenges." This simple shift in perspective was empowering. It reminded me that my thoughts hold incredible power, and I could choose to cultivate a mindset of resilience and faith.

The act of transforming my fears into prayers also deepened my connection to my intuition. I started listening more closely to the whispers of my heart. I began to notice patterns in my writing, recognizing themes that emerged over time. This self-awareness became a guiding light, helping me navigate the complexities of life with greater clarity.

One of the most profound lessons I learned through my prayer journal was the importance of surrender. I often found myself clinging to the need for control, wanting to dictate the outcomes of my prayers. However, as I wrote, I began to understand that true spiritual growth comes from letting go. I started incorporating prayers of surrender into my entries, acknowledging that I cannot always control the circumstances around me. I learned to trust the journey, to have faith that things would unfold as they were meant to.

One night, I found myself grappling with a particularly difficult situation that felt beyond my control. I opened my journal and poured out my heart, expressing my frustrations and fears. Then, I closed my eyes and took a few deep breaths. I wrote a prayer of surrender, asking for guidance and strength to navigate the uncertainty. I felt an incredible sense of relief wash over me as I released my grip on the situation. This act of surrender became a powerful turning point in my spiritual journey, allowing me to cultivate a deeper sense of trust in the universe.

As I continued to write, I also discovered the importance of community in my spiritual growth. I began to share snippets of my prayer journal with close friends, inviting them into my journey. I found that opening up about my thoughts and experiences fostered deeper connections. My friends would often share their own insights and reflections, creating a beautiful exchange of support and understanding.

One evening, I hosted a small gathering where we shared our intentions and prayers with one another. Each person took a turn reading from their journals, and I felt a profound sense of connection in that circle. It was a reminder that we are all navigating our unique journeys, yet we share common threads of hope, fear, and love. This experience reinforced my belief that prayer is not only a personal practice but also a communal one.

As I look back on my journey with my prayer journal, I am filled with gratitude for the growth and transformation it has sparked in my life. The pages of that journal hold the stories of my heart—the fears I've faced, the dreams I've nurtured, and the lessons I've learned. I've come to understand that prayer is a language of the heart, one that evolves and deepens over time.

My prayer journal has become a safe space for exploration, a place where I can be my true self without judgment. It encourages me to embrace vulnerability and authenticity, reminding me that spiritual growth is a lifelong journey. I continue to write, to explore, and to connect with my heart in ways that feel meaningful.

So, I invite you to consider the power of a prayer journal in your own life. Allow it to become a sacred space for your thoughts, emotions, and aspirations. Embrace the process of writing as a means of self-discovery and reflection. Whether you write daily, weekly, or whenever inspiration strikes, know that each entry holds the potential for growth and transformation. Let your heart speak, and watch as your journey unfolds in beautiful, unexpected ways.

The Power of Heartfelt Prayers

There's something profoundly intimate about heartfelt prayers. I've always believed that true prayer is a conversation, not a recitation. For years, I followed what I thought were the rules—structured prayers, repeated phrases, the same old words passed down through generations. But something changed for me when I realized that prayer wasn't about getting the words just right or adhering to some unwritten script. It was about connecting, heart to heart, with the divine. It was about being real, open, and vulnerable in that sacred space. It's strange how we sometimes forget that.

I remember a time when I felt utterly lost. My life had taken an unexpected turn, and I was struggling to understand how I ended up where I was. I didn't have the answers, and no matter how hard I tried to find clarity, everything seemed murky. I turned to prayer, but the usual words didn't seem to fit. They felt distant and mechanical, not aligned with the deep confusion I was experiencing. I realized then that I needed to throw out the script. I needed to speak from my heart, to say the things that I couldn't even put into neat sentences. That's when I began to discover the true power of heartfelt prayers.

It was a quiet evening, and I was alone in my room, feeling the weight of all the uncertainty. I sat down, closed my eyes, and for the first time in a long while, I didn't try to say the "right" words. I let the emotions flow. At first, it was hard. The silence felt awkward, and I wasn't sure where to start. But then I began to speak—softly, honestly, without pretense. I said things like, "I don't know what to do. I feel lost, and I'm scared. Please help me understand." And as I spoke, a sense of relief washed over me. I wasn't pretending to be okay; I wasn't reciting words I didn't feel. I was just being real.

That prayer didn't change my circumstances overnight. Life wasn't suddenly perfect. But what it did change was my connection to something greater than myself. I felt heard, in a way that I hadn't before. I felt like my struggles mattered, that they weren't just floating in the void. And that was the first time I truly understood the power of a heartfelt prayer. It's not about asking for miracles or instant solutions; it's about aligning our deepest selves with the divine presence that's always there, waiting for us to open up.

Another experience that cemented this understanding happened during a period of grief. I had lost someone close to me, and no matter how much time passed, the sorrow clung to me like a shadow. I couldn't shake it. The grief was overwhelming, and I didn't know how to express the depth of it. Traditional prayers felt inadequate, like they couldn't capture the rawness of what I was going through. So, I decided to speak from my pain. I remember sitting by a window, looking out at the rain, and simply saying, "I miss them so much. This hurts more than I can bear. Please give me the strength to carry this."

I didn't try to mask my grief. I didn't try to sugarcoat it with positive phrases. I just let it be what it was—deep, aching sorrow. And in that moment, I felt something shift. It was as if acknowledging the full weight of my pain in prayer allowed me to begin healing. I wasn't asking for the pain to be taken away, but for the strength to move through it. That was a turning point for me. It taught me that prayer doesn't have to be pretty or polished; it just has to be real.

Heartfelt prayers have become my way of navigating the ups and downs of life. They've taught me that I don't need to hide behind pretense when I'm speaking to the divine. I've had moments where I've cried during prayer, moments where I've laughed, moments where I've simply sat in silence because the words wouldn't come. And in all those moments, I've felt that same connection—the reassurance that my emotions, whatever they may be, are held in compassion and understanding.

One particular story comes to mind when I think about the power of heartfelt prayers. I was at a crossroads, unsure whether to pursue a new opportunity or stay in the comfortable routine I had built for myself. Fear held me back—fear of failure, fear of the unknown, fear that I wasn't good enough. I remember walking late at night, the cool breeze on my face, and praying aloud. I said something like, "I'm scared. I don't know if I can do this, and I don't want to make the wrong choice. Please help me find the courage to move forward, even if it's difficult."

That prayer wasn't just about asking for a solution. It was about confronting my fear, naming it, and inviting the divine to walk with me through it. And as I spoke those words, I felt lighter. The fear didn't disappear, but it no longer paralyzed me. I realized that the act of naming my fear in prayer had given me a sense of control over it. It wasn't running the show anymore. That's the beauty of heartfelt prayers—they give us a space to lay down the things we're carrying, to make sense of the emotions swirling inside us, and to invite a sense of peace, even when the circumstances haven't changed.

There was another time, a more joyful one, when I discovered that heartfelt prayers could also be about celebration. I had just experienced a major personal victory, something I had worked towards for years. The feeling of accomplishment was overwhelming, and I felt this deep sense of gratitude welling up inside me. Instead of offering a traditional prayer of thanks, I decided to write my own. I took out a journal and began to write, "Thank you for this moment. Thank you for every challenge that brought me here, for every lesson I've learned along the way. Thank you for giving me the strength to keep going, even when I doubted myself."

Writing that prayer was like pouring my heart onto the page. It wasn't just a list of things I was grateful for; it was an expression of the deep joy and fulfillment I was feeling in that moment. I realized then that prayers of celebration are just as important as prayers of petition or sorrow. They remind us to pause, to acknowledge the beauty and grace that exist in our lives, even amidst the struggles.

Over the years, I've come to see prayer as a dynamic, living thing. It evolves with us, changes as we change, and adapts to the unique experiences we go through. Heartfelt prayers aren't confined by rules or expectations. They're fluid, spontaneous, and deeply personal. Sometimes, they're long and reflective, and other times, they're as simple as a single sentence whispered in a moment of need. But no matter their form, they always carry the same essence—the raw, unfiltered language of the heart.

One of the most powerful aspects of heartfelt prayer is the way it brings us back to ourselves. In our busy, often chaotic lives, it's easy to lose touch with our innermost feelings. We get caught up in the hustle, in the need to be productive, in the pressures of daily life. But prayer invites us to slow down, to check in with ourselves, to ask, "How am I really doing? What do I need right now?" It's a moment of stillness in the storm, a reminder that we are more than the noise around us.

I've had moments where I've sat down to pray, thinking I knew what I needed, only to discover something entirely different. One evening, after a particularly stressful day, I sat down to pray for peace. But as I began to speak, I realized that what I was really feeling was not stress, but loneliness. I had been so busy, so focused on tasks and goals, that I hadn't taken the time to connect with others or with myself. So instead of asking for peace, I prayed for connection. I asked for the courage to reach out, to nurture the relationships that mattered to me, and to be more present with the people in my life.

That's the beauty of heartfelt prayer—it allows us to uncover the deeper truths that we might not even be aware of. It's a process of self-discovery, a way of peeling back the layers and getting to the heart of what we truly need. And in that process, we find healing, clarity, and strength.

Heartfelt prayers have also taught me the importance of surrender. There are times when no amount of effort or willpower can change a situation. In those moments, prayer becomes a way of letting go, of acknowledging that there are forces beyond my control. I've prayed through difficult times, asking for things to go a certain way, only to realize later that what I needed wasn't control, but trust. Trust that whatever happens, I will be okay. Trust that the divine has a plan, even if I can't see it in the moment. Those prayers of surrender have been some of the most transformative, because they've taught me to release my grip on the things I can't change and to find peace in the uncertainty.

As I reflect on my journey with prayer, I'm reminded of how much it has shaped my spiritual life. It has deepened my connection to the divine, but it has also deepened my connection to myself. Heartfelt prayers have become a way of honoring my emotions, my struggles, my joys, and my growth. They are the language of my heart, spoken in the most honest and raw way possible.

I don't think there's a right or wrong way to pray. I think the most important thing is to be true to yourself, to speak from your heart, and to trust that you are heard. Whether your prayer is a cry for

help, a shout of gratitude, or a quiet whisper in the night, know that it carries power. It connects you to something greater than yourself, to a love that holds you, listens to you, and walks with you through every season of life.

EPILOGUE

As we come to the close of this spiritual journey together, I want to express my heartfelt gratitude for your companionship along the way. Your willingness to explore these profound teachings on faith and prayer has been an integral part of bringing this book to life.

The journey doesn't end here. In fact, it's my hope that closing this book marks the beginning of a new chapter in your own spiritual exploration. The true measure of this work's value lies not in its pages, but in how it resonates within your heart and manifests in your life.

If the words and wisdom shared here have touched you, inspired you, or sparked a transformation in your spiritual practice, I would be deeply grateful if you could take a moment to share your thoughts with others.

Your voice matters. Your experience can light the way for fellow seekers on their own paths to wholeness. By sharing your insights, you become part of a larger conversation about faith, prayer, and spiritual growth.

I kindly ask you to consider leaving a review:

1. On Amazon: If you purchased this book on Amazon, your review there would be invaluable in helping others discover this guide.

2. On Goodreads: As a community of book lovers and thoughtful readers, your review on Goodreads can spark meaningful discussions.

3. On the platform where you purchased this book: Whether it was a local bookstore's website, Barnes & Noble, or another retailer, your review can

guide future readers.

4. On social media: If you feel comfortable, sharing your thoughts on platforms like Instagram, Twitter, or Facebook can help spread the word to your own community.

Your honest feedback, whether it's a few sentences or a more detailed reflection, can make a significant difference. It not only helps other potential readers but also provides me with invaluable insights that will inform my future work.

Remember, the most impactful reviews often share:
- How the book affected your personal spiritual journey
- Any specific practices or ideas that resonated with you
- How the book might benefit others on their path to wholeness

Lastly, if you found value in this book, please consider recommending it to friends, family, or anyone you think might benefit from its teachings. Word of mouth is a powerful way to share wisdom and foster a community of spiritual growth.

Thank you once again for being a part of this journey. May your path be filled with light, your prayers be answered, and your faith lead you to the wholeness you seek.

With boundless gratitude,

Nafeez Imtiaz

P.S. If you wish to continue the conversation or share your experiences directly with me, please feel free to reach out through my website or social media channels. Your stories and insights are always welcome and deeply appreciated.

AFTERWORD

As I pen these final words, I find myself sitting in the quiet of my study, surrounded by notebooks filled with scribbled insights, prayer beads from various traditions, and small tokens gifted by the many spiritual leaders I've had the privilege to meet. Each object tells a story, each a reminder of the profound journey that led to the creation of this book.

When I first set out to explore the world of prayer and faith, I could never have imagined the transformative impact it would have on my own life. What began as a quest for understanding has become a deeply personal odyssey of spiritual growth and self-discovery.

Throughout the process of researching and writing this book, I've been continually humbled by the generosity of spirit shown by the individuals I've encountered. From revered spiritual leaders to humble practitioners, each person I met opened their hearts and shared their wisdom with a grace that left me in awe. Their teachings have not only enriched the pages of this book but have also profoundly altered my own spiritual practice and worldview.

One of the most striking revelations of this journey has been the common threads that run through diverse spiritual traditions. Despite differences in language, culture, and specific beliefs, I found a universal yearning for connection – with the divine, with each other, and with our deepest selves. The methods may vary, but the destination seems remarkably similar: a state of wholeness, of peace, of alignment with something greater than ourselves.

I've come to understand that prayer, in its myriad forms, is not just a religious obligation or a way to petition for our needs. It is a powerful tool for transformation, a means of aligning our consciousness with higher truths, and a path to experiencing the interconnectedness of all things. Whether through spoken words, silent meditation, physical rituals, or acts of service, prayer has the potential to reshape our inner landscape and, by extension, the world around us.

As I reflect on the journey that led to this book, I'm filled with profound gratitude – for the teachers who shared their wisdom, for the experiences that challenged and changed me, and for you, the reader, who has chosen to engage with these teachings. My hope is that this book has not just imparted information, but has sparked a flame of curiosity and inspiration within you.

Remember, the words and practices shared in these pages are not meant to be definitive or prescriptive. They are invitations – invitations to explore, to question, to experiment, and to find what resonates with your own heart and spirit. Your journey to wholeness through faith and prayer is uniquely yours. Trust your intuition, be patient with yourself, and remain open to the unexpected ways in which the divine may speak to you.

As you close this book, know that in many ways, your journey is just beginning. The real work happens not in the reading, but in the living – in the daily choice to engage with your spirituality, to practice prayer in whatever form calls to you, and to continually seek that sense of wholeness we all long for.

I encourage you to take what you've learned here and make it your own. Adapt the practices, blend the teachings, create your own rituals. Let your spiritual life be a living, breathing thing that grows and evolves with you. And always remember that the ultimate goal is not perfection, but authenticity – a genuine expression of your unique connection to the divine.

Finally, I want to express my deepest gratitude to you, dear reader, for accompanying me on this incredible journey. Your willingness to explore these profound teachings and to consider new perspectives is a testament to the enduring human spirit of inquiry and growth. It's my sincere hope that this book has not only informed but also inspired you, challenging you to delve deeper into your own spiritual practice and to discover new dimensions of faith and prayer in your life.

As you move forward from these pages, may you carry with you the wisdom of the ages, the inspiration of diverse traditions, and the courage to forge your own path to wholeness. Remember, every prayer, every act of faith, no matter how small, has the power to transform – not just ourselves, but the world around us.

May your journey be blessed with moments of profound connection, unexpected insights, and the joy of discovering the divine within and all around you. And may you find, in your own unique way, that beautiful state of wholeness that awaits us all.

With deepest gratitude and blessings for your journey,

Nafeez Imtiaz

Milton Keynes UK
Ingram Content Group UK Ltd.
UKHW040256181024
449757UK00001B/64